INVISIBLE CITY

volumes in the collection of current poetry
edited by John McBride & Paul Vangelisti

1: *Humps & Wings: Polish poetry since '68*
2: *Italian Poetry, 1960–1980:
   from Neo to Post Avant-garde*
3: *Abandoned Latitudes:* new writing by three
   Los Angeles poets (Crosson, Thomas, Vangelisti)
4: *Invasions & other poems:* a selection of Antonio Porta
5: *Domain: works-in-progress* by G.T. James & Paul
   Vangelisti, with a sequence of photographs by Joe Goode
6: *Forest Beyond Nature:* verse & visuals by Emilio Villa,
   Giulia Niccolai & Luciano Caruso
0/7: *the first twenty-five (and then some):* the long-
   postponed anthology of the tabloid *Invisible City*

cover: LA ME GA SCRITO by Luciano Caruso
(1971, from a text by Emilio Villa)

Giulia Niccolai: SCULPTURE

FORESTA ULTRA NATURAM

"forest beyond nature":
verses & visuals by Emilio Villa,
Giulia Niccolai & Luciano Caruso
edited by Paul Vangelisti
translated by Pasquale Verdicchio,
Ippolita Rostagno & Paul Vangelisti

INVISIBLE CITY | 6
San Francisco & Los Angeles
1989

Copyright © 1989 by the Red Hill Press which reverts to the authors & translators upon publication.

Printing of this volume was funded by the California Arts Council. Special thanks to Anne Bourget for her patient assistance.

ISBN 0-88031-67-7
Library of Congress Number ? ? ? ?

Distributed by Small Press Distribution (Berkeley CA)

Occupying a vital place in Italian writing, these three poets are a passage between the historical and contemporary avant-gardes. In editing this collection, I could not help but be aware of the closing of a poetic argument — and perhaps of an historical moment — that had yielded a new definition of language both generous and antagonistic.

For now, when such terms as 'modern', 'post-modern', 'experimental' and 'avant-garde' appear at times contradictory, at times marketable self-parodies, here is a gathering of three poets whose work towards radical utterance remains provoking. With the usual limits of space and resources, I regret not being able to document the activity with which all three have complemented and reinforced their poetry: Villa's linguistic archeology, most notably his editions of Homer and the Old Testament; Niccolai's translations of Lewis Carroll, Gertrude Stein & many contemporary English-speaking writers; and Caruso's critical publications of visual poetry, particularly medieval Latin and Italian futurist texts.

I should close with a few more words about the crucial and enigmatic figure of Emilio Villa. In the present perspective, his work appears unique in the Italian avant-gardes. From the 1940s through the 1970s — especially in the politically inflamed post-War — Villa has been a paragon of experimentalism and internationalism for generations of writers (Niccolai and Caruso, to name only two). Restless and ever extensive, Villa's odyssey is uncompromising in the attempt to *exhaust* Italian poetic language. This collection, *Foresta ultra naturam* (the title of Villa's 1953 essay), might well be dedicated to him in honor of some 50 years of discovery.

— *Paul Vangelisti*

HYDRASOIL (1957)

*Poco è rimasto di quella nostra foresta ultra naturam,
lucus transiliens, foresta combattente; di quella nostra
giovinezza animata, poco; poche le conseguenze del nostro
nostro patronato assoluto; rare le punte di quelle altre
misure; peggio per gli altri; perché questo poco è solo
e tutto quel che è accaduto, qui, di vita generosa, di
spalancata Alleanza: dove filologia storia critica buro-
crazia quando vi metteranno le mani, paralitiche, trove-
ranno soltanto il nostro provocatorio, illimite, Niente.*

EMILIO VILLA

Little is left of our *foresta ultra naturam, lucus tran-
siliens,* combatent forest; little of our animated youth;
the consequences of our absolute patronage are few;
rare the points of those other measures; too bad for
the others; because this little bit is all and everything
that happened, here, of generous life, of wide-open
Alliance: where philology history criticism bureaucracy
when they will set their paralyzed hands on it they will
find only our provocative, boundless, Nothingness.

(trans. Pasquale Verdicchio)

(1964)

EMILIO VILLA

EMILIO VILLA was born near Milan in 1914. He is a seminal figure in the European avant-gardes as a bridge between the historical movements such as futurism and surrealism, and the neo-avantgardes of the fifties and sixties. From his first volumes of poems, *Ormai,* in 1947 (subtitled "pieces, compositions, antiphonies, 1936-1945") and *E ma dopo* in 1950 (subtitled "orations, compositions, formulas, 1943-1947"), Villa has pushed the limits of verbality to the apparent exhaustion of his native Italian. He has published many volumes of verse, visual poetry and other forms of experimental writing; as well as essays on literature and art, and several translations, most important being that of the *Odyssey* (1964).

This selection has been translated by Pasquale Verdicchio.

QUALSIASI LOMBARDIA

Stracco oramai di tirar dietro stinchi asciutti
per le corsie dei treni-merci, allora
mi porterò il mio senno sulle arsure dei furgoni
mortuari, carichi di ceri di fiorami di ricordi brutti,
incontro alle certose della luna, e voi vedrete
una mente coi tordi seminata sopra i campi
lombardi, dove un convoglio di fatui santuari,
negli acquitrini delle risiere in fuga,
perseguiterà fischiando il rimorso dei miei guai italiani:

dove l'ultimo parlar di noi civili, che si sa
che la città è fondata sopra sulla nostra nuca
e che, se il mondo casca, casca sulla nostra nuca, l'ultima
fantasia di restare in questa terra,
l'ultima vela, sono i vani, sono i lunghi
fiati blu, che veleggiano sopra la gelata, tra le palpebre
dell'occidente, verso le agrarie liturgie;
e magari là s'accenderanno in capo ai funghi
tutte le messe che lasciammo inadempiute, i piani
suonati nelle notti che rimangon da dormire nelle scapole.

Perché avevo specchiato la tonsura
della mia nuca alle trappole delle lune
più ragionevoli, nel rezzo delle rape.
Forse poteva un cardinale di Milano, il giorno
che nella porpora cisterna fogavano i miei occhi,
forse poteva intorno alle pubbliche fontane,
lì così in piazza, sui due piedi, battezzare un cane?

Bambino ho trafficato con onore,
con diligenza, sorridendo, nel seno delle oche
del mio paese; poi dal lago, nella cruna
poca degli occhi, d'incanto
sfiorirono i finocchi dietro un arcobaleno,
e i figli del popolo ridevano sotto gli oleandri:
dai boccioli, con la roggia lamentela
delle tarme, sui crespi capelli
il senso incolmabile scendeva della loro giovinezza.

Ho abbracciato una rondine nottetempo,
ardeva di portarmi, sotto ascelle,
l'odore dei miei fossi, e delle madri,

ANY LOMBARDY

Tired now of dragging behind dry shins
along the tracks of freight-trains, then
I will carry my wisdom on the feverishness of hearses,
loaded with candles wreaths bad memories,
toward the monasteries of the moon, and you will see
a mind with thrushes sown on the fields of Lombardy,
where a convoy of fatuous sanctuaries,
in the marshes of fleeing rice paddies,
will persecute the remorse of my Italian troubles, whistling:

where the last words of we civil ones, who know
that the city is founded on our skull, and that,
if the world were to collapse, it would on our skull,
the last fantasy of staying on this earth,
the last sail, are the rooms, are the long blue breaths,
that sail upon the frozen, between the eyelids of the west,
toward the agrarian liturgy;
and maybe there, before the mushrooms, will light
all the masses we left unfinished, the plans
played in the nights left still to sleep in the shoulder-blades.

Because I had reflected the tonsure
of my head in the traps of the most reasonable
moons, in the shadow of turnips.
Could a cardinal of Milan, on the day
that my eyes burned in the purple cistern,
maybe he could, around the public fountains,
there in the square, on two feet, baptize a dog?

A child, trafficked with honour,
with diligence, smiling, in the breast of the geese
of my land; then from the lake, in the small
of the eyes, from enchantment
the fennels withered behind a rainbow,
and the sons of the people laughed beneath oleanders:
from the buds, with the ditch-digging complaint
of the wood-worms, on the crimpy hair fell
the insurmountable sensation of their youth.

I embraced a swallow at nighttime,
it longed to take me, under its wing,
the scent of my ditches, and of the mother,

patito: voi mi avete confuso per uno
qualunque che i giunchi agitasse nelle cisterne.

Ma gli stracci del temporale ma gli stracci
alle frontiere dei tordi sventolati per allarme
volarono alle case con le vacche senza petti:
noi si pregava, coi calcagni giunti,
ad invocare sulle nostre ossa, il polverone
di tutte le bufere in alto al granoturco.

Se avete messo, sul pulpito, unti grembiuli di serva,
a salmodiare nel coro delle prevaricazioni,
a predicare sul teatro di certe sagrestie, manomesse
da manutengoli in foia e scalmanati,
voi che avete messo, sul pulpito, unti grembiuli di serva,
schernite le figlie di Maria durante le vermiglie
processioni: *oh candele istoriate
decalcomanie innocenti!*

Poi sfogliate, per piacere, le pagine dei morti,
ci rivedrete con i sandali del cristiano
nell'ora battuta dalla polvere, assunti
nell'ora dei santi e delle sante,
lungo l'elenco dei beati giornalieri,
vergini e martiri, vergini e confessori, vergini e ciarlatani.

E le volpi, le volpi, verecundia, sul muso
le volpi con lo sterco ci segnavano
già ieri le strade da infilare: odore secco
di strusa, e si partiva . . .
*Prendi la rocca e il fuso
e andiamo in California.*

A nuvole di nebbia dei re longobardi,
si partiva, per le cene, con le torce,
coi letti, arrugginiti, sulle spalle,
a fare una pasqua, per i morti,
senza tregua. E tramontava il giubilo
di pentecoste, a picco
sopra il torrente del mio paese,
una labile, unica Strona:

le donne, che ci avevan vigilato,
han volto, a capo in giù, le torce sante:
solo tre becchi di lampoda, a petrolio,

tolerated: you have mistaken me for one
who might stir up the junks in cisterns.

But the rags of the tempest but the rags
at the frontiers of the thrushes flapping
from warning flew to the homes with breastless cows:
we prayed, with ankles together,
invoking on our bones, the great dust-cloud
of all storms above the corn.

If you have placed on the pulpit
greasy maid's aprons to psalm in the choir
of prevarications, to preach on the stage
of certain vestries, violated by lustful
and hotheaded accomplices, you, who have placed
on the pulpit greasy maid's aprons,
scorned the daughters of Mary during
vermillion processions: *oh, historicized candles
innocent transfers!*

Then, please leaf through the pages of the dead,
you will see us again in Christian sandals
in the hour beaten by the dust, assumed
in the hour of all saints,
among the list of blessed laborers,
virgins and martyrs, virgins and confessors, virgins and charlatans.

And the foxes, the foxes, modesty, on the snout
the foxes with excrement marked
already yesterday the roads to take: dry smell
of silk fallings, and we were off...
*Get the spindle and distaff
and let's go to California.*

With clouds of fog of Longobard kings,
we left, for the dinners, with torches,
with beds, rusted, on shoulders,
to an Easter, for the dead,
without rest. And the jubilee of Pentecost
set, high above the torrent of my land,
a fleeting and unique Strona:

the women, who had kept vigil over us,
turned, head down, the sainted torches:
only three petrol lamp beaks,

ancora rischiaravano gli azimi
che si doveva trangugiare nelle albe
del bene e del male per le strade provinciali del luogo.

E ho preso, un giorno, lo stallo
nel rogo dei miei simboli privilegiati,
dove a scorze d'alberi, che la folgore brucava,
le foglie inaridite mi tiravano in ballo
le antifone più scrocche:

"Alza il tuo ferro contro il tuo petto,
perché si sappia fin dall'inverno,
se tu sei arido o fertile: e chi
ti salverà le dita dagli atti futuri?
chi avrà tenuto in custodia i tuoi guai italiani,
fino alla giornata del ritorno, *usque in diem?*"

"Non mettere il tuo cuore
sulla vigna di Sirtori o di Somma,
sulla vigna d'Appiano o di Missaglia,
perché l'agricoltore bagna il seme
dentro le brocche dell'aceto."

"Colui che implora, ogni mattino,
la pazienza agli acini dell'uva
saprà incendiare insieme
tutti i vigneti nel giorno dell'addio."

Zingari marinari personaggi intriganti
hanno sporcato i candidi damaschi,
i candelieri di ferro battuto e i busti al sidol:
ora non resta più che pelle e bava
per nutrire i paracarri delle strade secondarie;
ora sommessi nella fava del popolo ai piovaschi
i sepolcri potrebbero infiorarsi di bestiame regolato.

Però un giorno verranno alle vendemmie
(nel lume celeste la poiana e nella guerra
dei volti popolari e dentro i sessi riconosce
l'ora del transito rurale)
donne ostinate dalla Martesana,
gridando a piedi scalzi, per le angustie della lume.

"Noi volevamo seppellire i nonni
a grappoli folti, a grappoli satolli,

the azimuths were still clearing,
that we had to swallow in the dawns
of good and evil in the provincial streets of the place.

And, one day, I took a seat
in the stake of my privileged symbols,
where with tree bark that the lightning nibbled,
the dried leaves brought into it
the most cunning antiphons:

"Lift your iron to your chest,
so that it may be known from winter on
if you be arid or fertile: and who
will save your fingers from future deeds?
who will have kept custody of your Italian troubles,
until the day of return, *usque in diem?*"

"Do not place your heart
on the vines of Sirtori or of Somma,
on the vines of Appiano or of Missaglia,
because the farmer dips the seed
in vinegar jugs."

"He who implores, every morning,
patience to grape berries
will know how to set fire to all
the vineyards on the final day."

Sailing gypsies intriguing characters
have dirtied the candid damask,
the wrought-iron candleholders and the polished busts:
all that is left now is skin and dribble
to feed the posts of side-roads;
now subdued in the language of the people to squalls
the sepulchers could flower with regulated livestock.

For one day they will come to the grape harvests
(the buzzard in the azure light and in the war
of popular faces and inside the sexes recognizes
the hour of rural transit),
obstinate women of the Martesana,
barefoot and yelling for the anxious light.

"We wanted to bury our grandfathers
in thick bunches, in full bunches,

in grembo a quelle vigne" oppure
"De vinea viventium
asparagi e gardenie!"

Alla vendemmia fiorita di noi morti non satolli
portaci un vassoio di locuste in allegria,
impenitenti dal tempo del deserto.
Portaci un vassoio di locuste in allegria:
e ci ricorda che noi morti fummo guelfi
dalle ginocchia fino alle calcagna, e via.

Canteremo alla vendemmia,
tutte le montagne della diocesi danzando,
e dileguando i solchi e le carregge e i sassi
nel cuore incompiuto della brina "O barche,
eccetera, marcite lungo i fiumi di Babele,
alle paludi, tra i germogli di bambù,
illic flevimus ac stetimus
dum recordaremur tui, Sion"

E ritornando, zitto: rada l'aria,
(il cielo è in volo, in libertà)
si vedrà fino in fondo, in una fosca
vigilia di Sant'Ambrogio! Amalasunta
regina, dorme, in eirène, con i padri.
Tutto avremo dormito, come ladri,
vigilia di Sant'Ambrogio! Nella piazza
dove ancora si ragiona a due colori,
e i vicoletti sboccano a memoria, con alcune
mosche, a questa fiera impalpabile e segreta,
gli arcivescovi verranno a contrattare le trombette
di celluloide, i palloncini, e i craffen.

[1936, da *Oramai*]

in the bosom of those vineyards" or else
"De vinea viventium
asparagi e gardenie!"

At the proud harvest of us unsatiated dead
bring a platter of happy locusts,
unrepentant since the times of the desert.
Bring a platter of happy locusts:
and it reminds us that we were Guelphs
from our knees to our ankles, and so on.

We will sing to the harvest,
all the mountains of the diocese dancing,
and dispersing furrows and carts and stones
in the brine's incomplete heart "Oh boats,
etcetera, rotted along the rivers of Babel,
to the swamps, among the bamboo shoots,
illic flevimus ac stetimus
dum recordaremur tui, Sion"

And returning, quiet: parted the air,
(the sky in flight, free)
clear to the bottom, in a dark
Saint Ambrose's Eve! In the square
where arguments are still in two colours,
and the sidestreets open with memory, with some
flies, at this impalpable and secret fair,
the archbishops will come to negotiate
celluloid trumpets, balloons, and fritters.

[1936, from *Ormai*]

PEZZO 1940

E allora, ormai

quali reami e quante nuvole
negheranno nell'acqua vagabonda delle ronge, quante
in cima ai brughi fumeranno le cuccagne, e volti
sui marmi forti, e donne a fare i sughi sulle logge,
e messe cantate per formiche industri all'albeggìo,
con ostie nel lume del ciborio, santi
col gesso e le lavagne,
prima che la monotona crisalide si schiuda
ai dischi d'inusitate primavere, e porti
una ragione libera ed immobile: esse pietose
riveranno nell'intrigo degli azzurri sereni
senza che noi ce ne saremo neanche accorti.

E la secchia di verderame nel frattanto
dondolerà pendendo, senza culo: lunga
che non finisce più è la catena: sai perché
forse? Certi boccali anziani, sulle fiere,
la liturgia cattolica nel lume del ciborio,
come rosa piantata in alto a Gèrico . . .

Che imparo una fonetica accanita; ma non torna:
le lingue delle mucche sull'uncino nei macelli
non senza una indispensabile malinconia; e quell'adorna
maniera di sentire ciò che accada nei mastelli;
dentro l'occhio destro, senza che il sinistro nel suo sogno
veda, un timpano di piogge da prealpi, un nuvolo
di minestre di sopra le scodelle al mattino alla sera.

Ecco, ormai

Quale diocesi tra il bruito delle brianze e cieli d'indaco,
o sotto il fogliame dei dialetti, quali parrocchie
mireranno l'erba buona scintillare delle nostre
tibie, come le soneríe delle stazioni secondarie,
glicine e lume dei tuoi lampi, metalliche bufere
a pentecosti così rosse, intatte? Ormai

S'impara, e dìdici. E desso che ho potuto
baciare sotto i polsi malinconico profondo
il figlio dell'adultera, laddove Angera fresca
finta al nevischio d'alti turbini si nutre

PIECE 1940

And then, by now

which realms and how many clouds
will negate in the wandering water of ditches, how many
on the moors will snatch the prizes, and faces
on the strong marbles, and women making sauces at the lodges,
and masses sung for industrious ants at dawn,
with hosts in the lamp of the ciborium, saints
with chalk and blackboards,
before the monotonous chrysalis opens
to the records of unusual springs, and carries
a free and immobile reason: they will return
piteous to the intrigue of the calm azures
without our even being aware of it.

And the graygreen bucket will in the meanwhile
swing suspended, without a butt: so long
it never ends is the chain: do you maybe know
why? Some old jugs, on the fairs,
the catholic liturgy in the lamp of the ciborium,
like a rose planted on high in Jericho...

That I learn a dogged phonetics; but doesn't work:
the cow tongues on the hooks at the slaughter
not without an indispensable melancholy; and that fancy
manner of hearing that which happens in the wash-tubs;
in the right eye, so that the left does not see in its
dream, a tympanum of pre-Alpine rains, a clouding
of soups above the bowl in the morning in the evening.

Then, by now

What dioceses among the rustle of the Brianze and the indigo skies
or below the foliage of dialects, what parishes
will aim on the good grass sparks of our
tibulas, like the bells of country stations,
wisteria and lamp of your flashes, metallic gales
with such red pentecosts, intact? By now

We learn, and *didici*. And that I myself was able
to kiss under the wrists melancholy deep
the son of the adultress, there where Angera fresh
false to the sleet of high whirlwinds feeds

il caldo in segno dell'avida poiana,
si radunarono di prescia trasalendo le tendine,
nel palmo dei cortili: era già sera (così presto!
ah, così gelato), e il coltello piantato nella pesca.

Ormai

"Manda quell'umido calore delle tue poppe
di stiratrice, in cima agli altipiani"
ma mai nulla non si seppe al di là della ghirlanda
improvvisa dei tre corpi che si strinsero: un agguato.
E quel vago sentore del sapone e della cenere
alla fonda in mastelli, e lungo i canali
il muschio, lo zolfo sugli zoccoli, era schietto
sorseggio per i cani, per le nottole
che rondassero gelose: poi sul bordo della tavola,
tra le schegge e il vino spanto, disfregata
senza volere, la lucciola inscenava un'avventura.

Forse la nostra. Tu luna, coi rapidi partiri dentro in cuore
come una tovaglia sotto pioggia
(un timpano di pioggia dalle Azzorre)
pudica attenda, in corte, un Borromeo per dispute
superne d'amore e libertà
di popolo e repubblica perfetta,
tu balenavi inquieta sulle frange
degli scialli. E cortesia al tardo,

cortesia e conoscenza al lampaneggio
tardo nel palmo dei cortili. Nelle case
nostrane, con le porte spalancate ai responsori,
i ladri e i morti potevano girare e rigirare
liberamente, con tutta confidenza, tra un prosciutto
e il lardo, come un'ala di letàna! rigirare
e girare con stretta diligenza, dentro e fuori, guancie rase
dove una cosa d'aria che nessuno ascolta

E ormai

Muore nel soffio frigido delle poppe un vergognoso
sudore, e la brina vanisce sui ceppi di lattughe;
e un urlo sembrerà, di vetro, un urlo della luna
tutto che lasciammo succeder quella sera
fuori delle case nostrane, nelle musiche
rughe delle poiane senza tetto e senza nome.

the heat in the sign of greedy buzzards,
startled gathered hastily the curtains,
in the palm of courtyards: it was already evening (so soon!
oh, so cold), and the knife planted in the peach.

By now

"Send that humid heat of your laundress'
tits, to the top of the plateaus"
but nothing was ever known beyond the sudden garland
of the three bodies that held tight: an ambush.
And that vague scent of soap and ash
at the bottom of washtubs, and along the canals
the musk, the sulphur on the clogs, was pure
sipping for the dogs, for the owls
that would wander jealous: then at the border of the table,
among the slivers and the spilled wine, unwillingly
stimulated, the firefly played out an adventure.

Maybe ours. You, moon, with rapid bursts in the heart
like a tablecloth under the rain
(a tympanum of rain in the Azores)
modestly await, in court, a Borromeo for supernal disputes
on love and liberty
on the people and the perfect republic,
you flashed restless on the fringes
of the shawls. And courtesy to the late,

courtesy and knowledge at the late lightning
in the palm of courtyards. In our homes,
with the doors wide-open to the responsories,
the thieves and the dead could run around
freely, with all confidence, among the hams
and lard, like the wing of a lioness! run around
with tight diligence, in and out, shaved cheeks
where a thing of air that no-one listens to

And by now

A shameful sweat dies in the frigid breath of the tits
and the brine vanishes on the stalks of lettuce;
and a scream will seem, of glass, a scream of the moon
all that we allowed to happen that evening
outside our homes, in the musical wrinkles
of the nameless and homeless buzzards.

Pare così di prepararsi sempre, tra gli scandali
e i semplici doveri, come a sbarcare da una bicicletta
devastata dai lumi, dai fambros, dalle segale,
fremendo all'unisono noi due, colpa e talento,
per scopi e per ragioni differenti: questa vita!

[1939, da *Oramai*]

ASTRONOMY

Udito per caso sibilare la gran lancia viola nella ionosfera?

        poi transita di qui e sobrie aree
        dirama dai remoti seni e questo
        è questo il tuo parlare a trama
        questo essendo

l'opinione l'opera il respiro: non accorgersi confondere le acque

        etimi leggendari omologare nel suono
        di pietra pietra e nella conca alma
        del sinistro (piede o mano, ma sinistro)

udito i germogli decimati dalla calma ascia delle cadenze?
        un'opinione sì, ma un'opera è respiro.

          spazio
bene si crede che nello specchio lento delle rute si disfogli
          spirito

la fluorescente odissea dei gradi e le natantie mute
vertebre plenilunie declinate alla fonte delle proiezioni contrarie!
udito allora riverberare il suono nello screpolo universo
                della ionosfera?

So it seems a constant preparation, between scandals
and simple duties, as in getting off a bicycle
devastated by the lamps, by the raspberries, by the rye,
worrying in unison us two, guilt and talent,
for different reasons and scopes: this life!

                [1939, from *Oramai*]

ASTRONOMY

Heard by chance the great violent spear hiss into the ionosphere?

            then passes by here and sober airs
            issues from the remote breasts and this
            is this your talk in plot
            this being

the opinion the work the breath: to be unaware confuse the waters

            legendary etyms homologate in the sound
            from stone stone and in the basic soul
            of the sinister (hand or foot, but sinister)

heard the shoots decimated by the calm axe of cadences?
        yes, an opinion, but a work is breath.

                          space
it is well to believe that in   slow mirror of the rue unfolds
                          spirit

the fluorescent odyssey of grades and barges and mute
full-moon vertebrae waned to the source of contrary projections!
heard the sound reverberate in the broken universe
                          of the ionosphere?

GEOGRAFIA

Sconfina, forma reale, nella balugine arsa delle chiome
inanimate! eludi il nome! penetra

il nesso fantastico delle matematiche particolari: e sparsa
furia di là là dove la tempesta

musica nidiate di appennini e i verecondi

nerbi delle foci essenziali
e dei congegni librati a larghi schemi nell'anello

continentale e dei coefficienti
di vili radici, percettibili

appena nella sinossi fiorita, e il sesso stralunato e delle pleiadi,
gentili narici sottovoce

DINAMICA ACCANITA

A mente formuliamo una dinamica
accanita: il carro con le cinque ruote
oblique nel senso periodico
dei punti cardinali sulle dita della mano usuale.

E se tu vedi adagio salire per la china storta
questa grande ruota morta, bene, sèguila
pari pari, e giunto in alto sui ripiani panoramici

e tu ruba dalle matte arene del silenzio geloso
nell'ora che la porta litargica, gl'illimiti
itinerari e spazi vulnerabili recuperando, sbatte
sullo stipite e nel cardine di sale

cigola accanitamente, quel che alla terra torna
misurato compenso e quota infera
ideale: ruba

corna gentili di sangue congolese, e la luna
inviperita sulle cateratte.

[1950, da *E ma dopo*]

GEOGRAPHY

Trespasses, real form, into the dry flash of foliage
inanimate!   evade the name!   penetrates

the fantastic bond of particular mathematics: and sparse
fury there   there where the storm

music swarms of Appenines and the bashful

nerves of essential mouths
and of contraptions gliding in grand schemes in the ring

continental   and of coefficients
of vile roots,   perceptible

barely in the blossomed synopsis, and the distraught sex and Pleiades,
gentle nostrils   sottovoce.

PERSISTENT DYNAMICS

We formulate persistent dynamics
in our heads: the cart with five wheels
oblique in the periodic sense
of cardinal points on the fingers of the usual hand.

And if you see this great dead wheel climb slowly
the crooked slope, well, follow it along,
and having reached on high panoramic terraces

and you steal from the mad sands of jealous silence
in the hour that carries it, unlimited
itineraries and vulnerable spaces recuperating, slams
against the jamb and into the salt hinge

squeals persistently, that which returns to the earth
measured compensation and infernal quota
ideal: steal

gentle horn of Congolese blood, and the moon
furious on the cataracts.

[1950, from *E ma dopo*]

COMIZIO MILLENOVECENTO 53

sede di od rosa maglia di anice di grappa e di naftalina, e odore
di fegato di merluzzo e di carogne nel vestibolo delle narici e lungo il torace
brivido d'incenso, trame fischiate di camole di arredi nella foresta sottogonna del corpuschristi,

uguaglia l'incanto incendiato dei Patti Massimi: oh, albero
di avvenenza Speleofonica, albero del Precetto, di ladra
cideia, di fonda chiacchera, che il sangue in Itaglia* non lava
le soglie e i marciapiedi, ma il chianti su uno straccio di tovaglia nunziale
appena che libato impiastra di rosso il sale e le freguglie di pane, e il coppino, buon augurio,
che sa la goda a darci dentro! e uno allora, diceva la rava e la fava, e che, eh no, eh no,
 eh no, eh no!
 eh si, sociofugo
 eh, assimilatore
se ghe scapa la caca de sgnapa ghe se scepa la ciapa del bus del cu, del peritoneo! e uno allora

 per Due Coltelli e Tre in fondo al lago inan ellato nei laceri
 ragiona a gran fatica in mezzo ai sassi sybillini tovaglia, con i crampi
 bindelli della celeste ai dieci nudi
 e il gomito che scotta quando per i campi scaglia ai dieci e innescata è la sera:
 venti la fionda verso dove non ci si vede più

ma: albero geodetico, fiuto dello stratempo fedele, albero di galeotta
avvenenza, negli scudi che il nubilo, sù e giù, sparpaglia, e tempo
stravagante, a spasso, siù e giù, sulle finestre sulle croste sulle tibie sopra i cuoi sopra il lattime
delle guance nella cagliata e nella coppa a fare opachi stampi e malinconica

COMIZIO MILLENOVECENTO 53 (Comizio Nineteen53)

place of odd rose stitch of anise of grappa and moth-balls, and odors
of cod liver and carrion in the vestibule of the nostrils   and along the thorax
chill of incense, whistled plots of wood-warms of vestments in the forest underskirt of corpuschristi,

equals the fired enchantment of the Patti Massimi: oh, tree
of Spelaeophoric loveliness,   tree of the Order of   thief
eideic, of small talk, that the blood   in Itaglia*   does not wash
thresholds and sidewalks,   but the chianti on a rag of a nuncial cloth
barely tasted smears the salt of red and the crumbs, and the ladle, good luck,
may he enjoy giving it his all! one then, said the radish and the bean, and what, oh no, oh no,
                                                                                                        oh no, oh no!
                                                                                                        oh yes, sociopath
                                                                                                        oh, assimilator
if you feel the grappa shit runnin it might spoil the asshole's cheek, of the peritoneum! one then

                for Two Knives and Three at the bottom of the con centric lake   in the lacerations
                reasons with great effort among the sibylline stones   table cloth, with cramps
                bindle of the heavenly   to the ten naked
                and the elbow that burns when in the fields throws to the ten
                winds the slingshot toward the place where one loses sight   and evening has taken the bait

but: geodetic tree, smell of faithful excess time,   tree of galliot
event, in the shields that the clouds, up and down, spread   and time
extravagant, walking, up and down, on the windows on the scabs on the tibias on the skins
of the cheeks in the curds & in the cup to make opaque stamps   and melancholy

*Play on 'Italy' and the verb 'cut' or 'incise'.

[27]

carezza e lente spire, e dura scorza alle gibigiane: rotta, così
sgargia la livella del T e B: e domani, ma domani,   il candore
che entra come un temperino nudo, come una carognata, la gemma della paura o dello sfizio, un gotto
di manduria dentro il lago, e ma domani sarà una gran bella giornata! un gemito
dentro i testicoli, lungo, e nostalgia della sua cenere   e ma domani

    più nisciuno in questa scura foppa sa più bene se la pietra permansiva
    e immemore in immemore equilibrio starà sopra la pietra,
    o sull'arcata delle spalle i pensamenti a grani con tutta
    quella catabrega di figlioli a precipizio   e la legge
    dell'uomo che ha mangiato di straforo il pànico vitale, sussidio
    delle comunità, delle fabbricerie, dei sindacati, delle tribù . . .

    tarlate da un acume propizievole   e il lume
    sforbiciato da molteplici scaramanzie, come l'albero
    ignaro, svelto   nel rameggio
    tra il nubilo e il tempaccio nazionale e internazionale, il frullo
    e la chiarezza in equilibrio immemore, una fetta   di buontempo,
    fluttuando   e l'ecumene

    dei bulbi pieno e vuoto vidima il potere e il nonpotere dell'Onnipotente
    genuino, alleato al tenero delirio dell'inedia e allo schianto
    furtivo, elegiaco, delle erotiche asce, e degli stipiti deperiti a colpi d'anca,
    e sbatti e molla e lasciandare che il cielo   appartiene!

e nelle rocce di tenebre ti si strozzano i lividi precipizi le siderée fiumane i rari
riflessi   per somme linee   e i prèsaghi
tedeum   e l'unghia incarnata delle estasi dentro le cortecce
del gelso   e l'occhio estirpato alla sua roccia, immoto

[28]

caress and slow sighs, and hard crust to the mirror flashing   broken, like this,
shows off the level of the T & B: and tomorrow, but tomorrow,   the candour
that enters like a naked jackknife, like a stinker, the gem of fear or of the hell of it, a goblet
of manduria in the lake, but tomorrow will be one hell of a nice day!   a moan
in the testicles, long, and longing for its ashes   but tomorrow

               t'ain't nobody in this dark hole knows anymore if the impermeable rock
               and immemorial in immemorial equilibrium will stay on the rock,
               or on the arch of the shoulders the thoughts in grains with all
               that hurly-burly of sons in precipice   and the law
               of the man who ate hungrily the vital panic, subsidy
               of the communities, of vestry-boards, of unions, of tribes. . . .

                              eaten by a favourable acumen   and the lamp
                              scissored by multiple sorceries, like the tree
                              unaware, quick   in the branches
                              between the clouds and the bad national and international weather, the whirl
                              and the clarity in immemorial equilibrium, a slice   of nice weather,
                              fluctuating   and the ecumene

                                             of bulbs full and empty is validated the power and powerlessness of the Omnipotent
                                             genuine, ally to the tender delirium of tedium and to the crash
                                             furtive, elegiac, of the erotic axes, and of the jambs withered by hip blows,
                                             and slam it and let go and let it be that heaven   belongs!

and in the stones of darkness your bruised precipices choke the sidereal streaming the rare
reflexes   by major lines   and the foreboding
tedeums   and the ingrown nail of ecstasy in the bark
of the jasmine   and the extracted eye at its stone, immobile

[29]

sugli oziosi scandagli, ebete vedetta   fino a che
la fanfara di carruba intonerà a pelo d'aria, scrocchiando,   l'era nuova,
l'era bicipite, delle diavolerie fonetiche,   i neumi palinsesti
dal foro dell'uovo di una syllaba clandestina solitaria esimia tenue caduca urbana generosa
lunga e carnale come il corpus della separazione e dell'uguaglianza: e nella cuna
tonda, come dei due orecchi del manzo, del padiglione dell'orecchio tra timpano e martelletto
rugando, fiorisce il cembalo insonne lanceolato degli espressi di frontiera, e il polverone
stormendo si avventa fuori orario dei camion, e il senso, a distanza,
delle luci gemelle nelle orecchie, perpetuo, sommesso attimo   e baleno
dei Novissimi: cioè, una vallata, a canestri, di albe   immolate
dall'amor delle anime, dal suffragio   indenne
delle larve e dei cognomi pellegrini oltremondani barbari nazionali necessari sovietici o giudei
uno che incomincia così, che finisce cosà,   darà agli incendi
l'Uccello di apollo e le cosce di santa Creatura, maschia o femmino,

   oh, ignaro, oh gelido oh decrescente talamo dei nostri aliti
   a ridosso, scapola a scapola! omelia e smalto e muscolo
   del sortilegio paraclitico, esalando, in virga verbi,
   ti fulmini, o sancta ecclesia, novero ecumenico, informe
   apocalisse vocalizzata e suggellata con labbra inerti, tra le vigne
   ti fulmini: uno stupore idologico, ma maligno, e una rissa
   aspra di cieli incenerisca il satanico peplo, il pascolo e il nubifragio

                                                                                                    [1953, da *Comizio Millenovecento* 53]

on the idle sounders, obtuse lookout   until
the carob fanfare intones in a breath of air, crackling,   the new age
the bicipital age, of phonetic sorceries,   the palinsestic neums
from the hole of the egg of a clandestine syllable solitary eminent slight fleeting urban generous
long and carnal like the corpus of separation and equality: and in the cradle
round, like the two steer ears, the outer ear between eardrum and hammer
bothering, flowers the sleepless tambourine leanciolate of the border expresses, and the dust storm
storming blows when the trucks don't run, and the sense, in the distance,
of the twin lights in the ears, perpetual, subdued moment   and flash
of the Novissimi: in other words, a valley, in bushels, of dawns   sacrificed
by the love of the souls, by the suffrage   undamaged
of the larvae and of the pilgrim surnames ultramundane barbarous national necessary sovietic or jewish
one that begins like this, that ends like that,   will give the fires
the Bird of Apollo and the thighs of saint Creature, biy or gorl,

oh, ignorant, oh cold oh diminishing thalamus of our breaths
together, shoulder to shoulder! homily and enamel and muscle
of the paracletic sorcery, exhaling, *in virga verbi,*
you fulminate yourself, *o sancta ecclesia,* ecumencial number, formless
vocalized apocalypse and sealed with inert lips, among vineyards
you fulminate yourself: an idolatrous stupor, but malignant, and a dispute
harsh of skies incinerate the satanic peplum, the pasture and the downpour.

[1953, from *Comizio Millenovecento53*]

THAT WHICH IS PRIMITIVE

(We search for a balance that aesthetical culture has spoiled if not altogether ruined)

Even before declaring our dangerous nostalgia for prehistoric recreations and ethnographic materials, we must describe its romantic quality, its decadent origins, its literary circumstance and aesthetical torpor that set it on its way and brought it to us, like a type of aristocratic and private infection.

This nostalgia became a poetics. Then, on rebellious ground it became a tool for work or idleness, in which irony was dominant, undoing all the good aesthetic intentions in a loud and deaf emptiness: hygenic perhaps, even if menacing. We ourselves were ready to receive with anxious hands the ethnographic and paleohistoric contents that had burst onto the art scene, upsetting the results of romantic stupidity, but above all creating an island in the cultural lake. In fact bourgeois culture, in its elaborations of a critical nature, as much idealistic as positivistic, relegated to a deaf position all the materials that archæology discovered and catalogued, and reacquired through travels to the lands of protohistoric cultures: science carried out, as it still does with admirable attention, its statistical, inductive, comparative task. But the official critics denounced (and continue to) with a contemptuous gesture, the "ethnography" of these artifacts. Splendid artifacts of a great historical shipwreck: and the avantgardes of melancholy and of splendid infantilism, according to the dominant poetics, and all the "archaisms", seized them without any criteria, for a transport that was in one sense purely physical, and in another sense purely aesthetic. What did Willendorf's Venus have more human or less human than Cyrene's Venus? What emotional value did the Maori mask or Benin idol have when placed alongside the statues of the Naumburg cathedral? And was not a Cromlech more intense and spasmodic than the Parthenon or Bernini's colonnade? Between the disorderly and polemic marvel of the former (full of spirit and hope) and the systematic obstinance of official criticism, narrow & still stubborn, there was not even a worthwhile dispute, but only reciprocal contempt. The static elaboration of the concept of art on the basis of late idealistic & positivistic culture (especially Italian, with its unwise delays, provincial, marginal, sultry), didn't even have the satisfaction of figuring out what was happening. On the other hand, the poetics of archaism, in a certain way, related to the exoticism of the previous century (of Delacroix, for example; or of Van Gogh's and Toulouse-Lautrec's orientalism) remained rather astonished and content with its ideologies, perhaps superficial, but polemically sensational. An affirmation of independence, of freedom before the general foolishness of idealistic criticism, was certainly useful and interesting. It only lacked a concrete spirit, and organization; and it did not cease to be amateurish even in the hands of Modigliani, or of Picasso, Brancusi, Klee, Kandinsky, Mirò or Arp. They searched for stylishness, forms and formulas, impressions and motivations, themes and fossilized tastes, images of confused dreams and scraps of unseen purity, fragments and pieces of hallucinations, brief evasive releases, reconstructions of dead hypothesis, symbols and magic, spectral affairs. As if to scratch the underneath of a thick crust a formal conscience without history, instantaneous and esterified, unpublished amusements; in substance, the search for a new literary patrimony. These Stevensons, these Conrads of the figurative trade, pirate melancholy with phosphorescent hands, produced at the end a squalid panorama of subtle formal obscurities, of stimulating dogma that were nevertheless lacking historic contact.

But now that the horizons and the very soul of the figurative trade have been enriched with free instincts, with gestures, with encounters, and with overall health; now that official thought has diminished in officiality and has become more and more inadequate, this could be the time to really take possession, humanly, with active conveyance, of those worlds that are all but fantastic and should be simply considered human, continuous expressions of intelligence and desire: absolute coherence of work and reality and not simple models through which to express one's personality.

Now would be the time to extend this great bridge to the past, meaning the future. To subtract from improvisation, from emphasis and from literature all production. It comes down to affecting, on the whole of the salvaged and compared materials, the idea, the substance: the reason for figurative culture. It comes down to a reacquisition of the evidence and the organic continuity, almost biological, of necessary human actions: and by human and necessary is meant all that has root and document expressed in the ground of all people in time and the structural unity of the variants and comparisons. Raise this system as a counterweight (or as a mirror) to the continuous descent towards the depths that belong to the impulses of intuition, of the spontaneous evocation, of the personal impulses, and of the unstoppable invasion of literary revelations easily soluble in the orgy, in delirium, in vacancy.

First of all, it is possible to suppose that it is a duty to indicate to the visual arts the task of setting up premises for a new culture, one that will be very human, mainly human and not humanistic, at least in the sense that it would raise our opus to a level higher than the vulgar one established by the official culture. That is not culture as we would want it, but an arid form made up of a sociological level so and so determined, already definable in its dynamic of little potential. The boring predicators of aesthetics are to be considered the most noxious insects of our development. Aesthetics is the most deformed and apparent condition of official culture.

[from ARTI VISIVE 4/5, Rome, May 1957]

UN EDEN PRÉCOX : LOGOGRAMMATA (1957)

ASH OVERRITVAL

to Philippe Lamantia
Horroris causa
        LUQSOR
Numembre — Decendre 1964

HUR (to phil hippe la mentia)

Sexual Hurrican uper the BayDay of the BayDay or
        sur le glan de l'ecoute
        sur le glande de l'echouté
        lesffâmmes dénoncent le diaggramme du
        toitu

et Toitu dyeux maudits Sexual Spitfire Sexual Hurrican
Toitu Soft Trinity   Parouusie porquoi
pourquoi dje dyeu, Toitu ne m'a pas consigné la langue de la liberté?
        Imaginalsexuat, Thermotheogamic Day! au moins souffle
and what, And what by what, what by, what wy and whatwhat,
christ my christ and you, strip, corre salta cacamangia, and you
you whatwhat? what wasting? and you   but
uwhat?!   foodr-gathering,
fouillefouille fouille fou fui!   and
alla is what   all of all is what of what)   (what of you
what of here   what of everywhere   what of allall
whot off   dip into
meme   me   commext   e   undefined queachy but
        put   it   ut
        then   it   is   it
        and   at
        it is Am
        hor ho horolohole!
navybeans navybirds navytrees navyyear   whoho! who
undefined queachy but   tempêtre incon
        nu

traité — rituel

    (prendre p r e n d r e   prendre re!
        prendre
        pour
  pren   dre   pa)

in !   Painfoundre, Painfoutre !   (Foudre Inconcevable sur
Ciel Sec sur où sur oùhoùh sur mortepluie sur temps crû, `!
(sur. . . . .   )   (tu
sais questcequecest que SAIETTA ? saetta?) selemnelle
soleil mnelle, elle l'arcade, amour, épouse famililière
le feu est parti, le feu est, parti, pour rendre pain brûlé —
pain!) qui subsiste dernier phosphehaine — prenez prenez donc
pain langueoisse d'eaux   d'eaufeu   en cage
tous les verres subtiles sur chaudeterre, aù morc eaux
de feu de foi où morc eaux de foudre de feu, d'où ?   qui
qui part en s'arrachant . . . . . . laisse-moi couler mêler l'oroule,
eh, luhune?   lu   ne) ah, majesté pleine, ma jesté
à peine, oh   pommes aux pommes eaux lèvres
(plonge   lequel   ardence   ence   envahihit
et jette dans   le   coeur   due   serpent)
tu réponds   tu réponds ?   tu   texplores
tu   tu texplores donc oublies toublies   donc ? (
)donc ; couche donc, de férocité, touche délicatasse apparue, glissée,
spiralespry abbatue dans le jenesuispas, non, je ne suis pas(
(dont un jour ! (et le sommet s'égaille, long,
                          (et rénait d'une croûte
(et tourne   et rejaillit
               et   les pieds en ronde autour dei soi
                                               se dérobent
              ⟶   orbe tortyeux   au tour du monte
(clous,   clous periballein, clouclous, colus, ah, tentacules-yeux
                                       autour de la borne
louche louche !   bourrue !   (?) poupe rêtée !   assassin !
                                       pour les yeux-grives
                                       pour y puiser pour y goûter
                                       ton oeil? sous les averses
                                       rouges, bien, chaque trou
est préopice tout ouvert à l'archer   ton trou ? bien,
oh, Saindémon propuce à toutes
oeuvreprières !)   (précipicyeux, près !)
                                        (imâge glissée !
(à toute entreprise sereine) bien, chaque huncère est propice à tout
tourbillon   trous pribàllein   trous vexés, comme pur tremper
ce qui a du poids dans une autre chose qui n'en a pas qui
n'en a plus   (sup(p)lex usu rpatrix)   (baisez l'egypte!)
(biasez l'égypte) avant de combattre ttre, de travailler sur son
                                       propre nom,

[37]

et le tuer, tu es le nom, et de délibérer avec des dents à scie,
les dents disparus, les frissons-pipilotes dans la petitesse galactique...
petite sse, spry

étu de Reljigion Incomparée: trâitré long
Palinpseste d'Herbes: à tout autre titre.

(de meme me   ) (de même que de queues   d'eux
que d'eux d'aux demême   que me)
                              (puisqué l'Essentiel
du Tout Distinct est Sujet d'eux Resonances)
(et que   foisonnant de twiste les pingouins
se présentèrent) (les Pigeons   se   rebaptisent!)
(deux Visiteurs, d'un voix belle longue, d'une langue
                              e a, d'une voile
ongle   d'une solitude telle   ongle de solitude extensive!
            (même ils alternent dissous exchalés
             la barbe est   et begave, zagaia)
            (et huhurlele le dieu   huhurle le voeu qu'il
                 à merveille   d'audace à mer)   dessine
(le longlelesjunglesdlinoui   (le Religioni   scompagnate)!
                 (Viseur! . . . .)
            depuis l'aurigine des Saveurs dyeux Sauveurs!)
(le longlalanguerinouis lelongle lelonglalongeurdinoui lelong!
enraciné: l'orgeuil: la solitude des dyeux dans la lassitude alter-
                                        nelle au fond
autelernelle haute auh!   (bagarre!)   (vacarme!)   et
s p o t a t o e s   d'afriquer   r h y t h m e s
nikeur   nike   niketé (dit par diato) (di à d'eau!)
(eux-eux . . . . . .eux, vraiment!) (qui se trémoussent) eh, le
chrome   (euh, quel!   et puis hur hurdur de dureté, aoh!)
                              que relles è normes!)
   (et les oeufs des herbes deserts discrets lentement   ça me plut
    les oeufs de la t o t a l i t e é   se e hurtent
    les oeufs s'abreuvent   et où s'abreuvent le Rameurs?
    Râ, bien, Râ Ra meurt, ehinh! eux il se cuisent se cuisent
    la Reine incroyable impalpable du Psychique   (Savoureur!)...
                                             (Sauveur
en arrière, twistez, twistètez! abominez! abhominez! nénez!)
(délicate   cate   incorrompue   légendeparachute
à la dep stance inexprimée sous tous les reins rognonbouches

[38]

) spus les rondes   caressent
                          les identesités
                               préconceptionnelles
des Forces Enaniméés à l'heure Juste
oeufrintellige ance once ence interleg lig
échec de douceur!
) telle   moue   dique
                            ve
                          ment
                      tels les mots pris au sens du MasSacre!)
(même acte interrompu incorrompu incontenu
                qu'un Monstre
                sans pitié
                détruit
                à quoi bon;
                à quoi bon?   (
arbitraire parti culière ment   cet   aspect di scrupehuhule
)
   et, oh, les échos suprêmes!)   (qui creusent) (qui cr   eux)

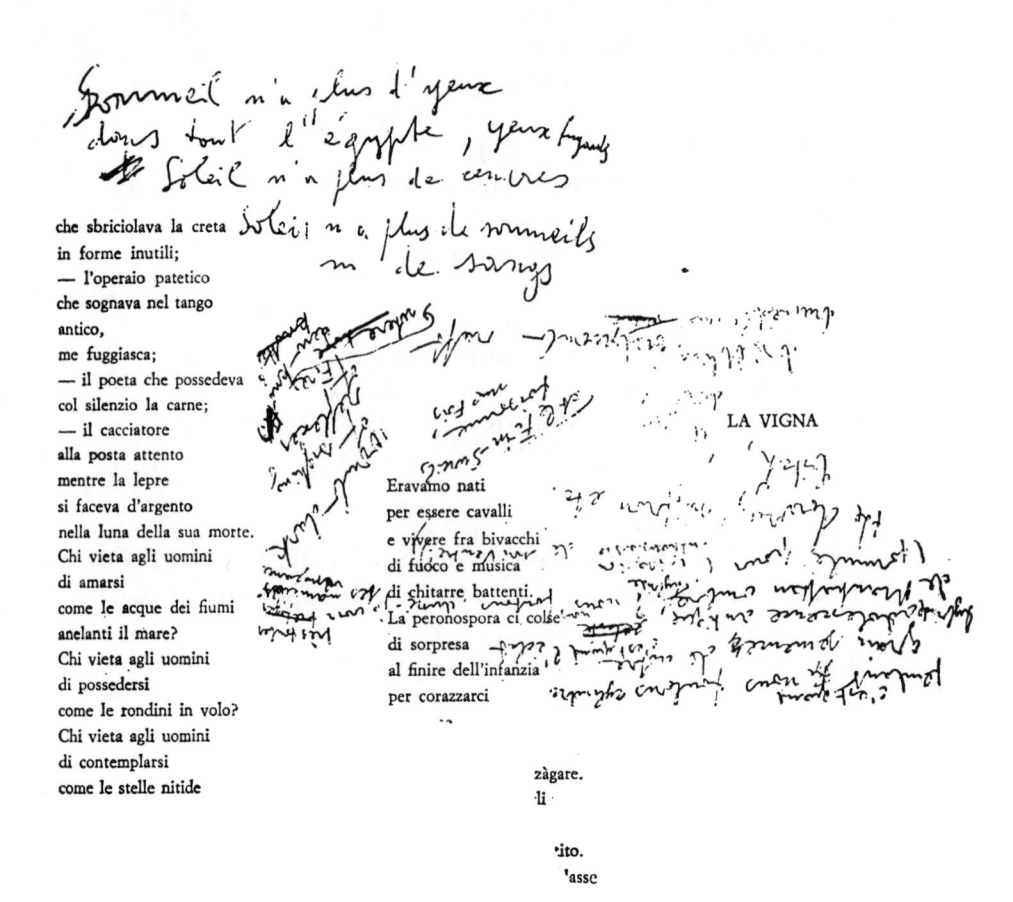

che sbriciolava la creta
in forme inutili;
— l'operaio patetico
che sognava nel tango
antico,
me fuggiasca;
— il poeta che possedeva
col silenzio la carne;
— il cacciatore
alla posta attento
mentre la lepre
si faceva d'argento
nella luna della sua morte.
Chi vieta agli uomini
di amarsi
come le acque dei fiumi
anelanti il mare?
Chi vieta agli uomini
di possedersi
come le rondini in volo?
Chi vieta agli uomini
di contemplarsi
come le stelle nitide

LA VIGNA

Eravamo nati
per essere cavalli
e vivere fra bivacchi
di fuoco e musica
di chitarre battenti.
La peronospora ci colse
di sorpresa
al finire dell'infanzia
per corazzarci

zàgare.
·li

·ito.
'asse

SOMMEIL : LA VIGNA (INEDITO) (1967)

HISSE TOI RE
D'AMOUR DA MOU RIRE

Romansexe
par Emilio Villa

Sixieme Edition
MCMXXI

> *encore une fois ce livre droits*
> *de traduction et de reproduction*
> *réservés pour tous pays qui font*
> *l'amour, y compris la su ede,*
> *la norv ède et le dan   mark*

I soirée

      les lèvres
      aveugles
      devenues

lèchent

le (les) (1) pierres-ensembles   ont di que tu es tu
lèche les lèvres du christianisme
        une Crampe Charnelle in corpore luteo

II soirée

                                                                                              SEE SAW
                                                                                              FACE TONE
                                                                                              PEDERSTALS
                                                                                              THROAT
                                                                                              BATTOM
                                                                                              SLEE EEP!

qu'   elle   ignore(ra)

             ce

qu'est devenu son

        Géniteur

             aux diles tordues

                  ju vén îles

                l'Incarnation qui mente se meurt
                (se mord, mordre) (se merde) dans
                son dedans, du son (je se mords)
                (suis donc) (je suis mords)
                (corpor and)
                          (la toute étée, elle)

                                                                                             BED CHICKENS
                                                                                            BED CHICKENS
                                                                                             BED CHICKENS

un troubli troutotal
pénétrant, en salive refusée

[42]

III soirée

        ne suis-je donc que   ?

                (ou en)

mais elle ne se verra foutre
soi-même   , soi l'autre,
dans la Vulve Plénaire,
Vulve Pleurante Etern   elle,

                mi   roir

que quoi?   où   a?   hein?

quoi rien?

(et le Déordorant
Vulvemachie
sur la Sommité
Perpetuum)

                    IV soirée

TO BE SEEN

          (ma proie
           (ta troie, 3)
          (ma toi,
             onde !)

LA ME SCRITO (Villa & Caruso, 1971)

(turn page 45 clockwise):
PLASTICO TELICO (1974)

PERIODO CENOTELICO
PERIODO ISOTELICO
POLMONE GALASSICO
SABBIA COSMICA
VERTEBRA MAGNETICA
PERIODO OLOTELICO
ABISSO PLEROCENOSI

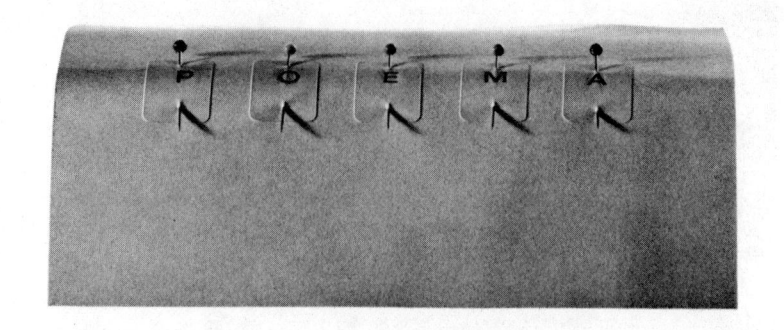

PINNED-DOWN TEXT

GIULIA NICCOLAI

GIULIA NICCOLAI was born in Milan in 1934. After a career as a photojournalist, she published a novel, *Il grande angolo,* in 1966. Associated for many years with the review, *Tam-Tam,* she published several volumes of poems (linear, visual/object, and nonsense lyrics) with Edizioni Geiger: *Humpty Dumpty* (1969), *Greenwich* (1971), *Poema & Oggetto* (1974) & *Russky Salad Ballads & Webster Poems* (1977). A selection of poems, *Harry's Bar e altre poesie, 1969-1980,* was published by Feltrinelli in 1981; *Singsong for a New Year's Adam & Eve* appeared in the most recent tabloid issue of *Invisible City* (July 1982). Verlag Droschl published, in German, her *Frisbees* (1986). The *Frisbees,* excerpted herein, are forthcoming from Mondadori.

Niccolai has published numerous translations from English and American literature, most notably Lewis Carroll's *Jabberwocky* and Gertrude Stein's *Geographical History of America* (Milan: La Tartaruga, 1980).

This selection has been translated by Paul Vangelisti, with her assistance.

POSITIVO & NEGATIVO

Ogni cosa può accadere
avere un senso o non averlo.

Non ha verità da proporre
mantiene aperto il significato
il senso nasce nominando le cose.

Un'impaginazione
una comunicazione di forme
l'ipotesi di una realtà in movimento:
una vertigine di inversioni
infinite e diverse.

E ciò che ad esse si oppone
può essere sempre rovesciato:
nel proprio contrario.

IL SOGGETTO È IL LINGUAGGIO

Un'idea di rivalsa: la rappresaglia
o la vendetta della parola pensata
(compiere il gesto di inventarsi una lingua
compiere l'atto con cui ci si appropria del linguaggio).

Anche se contigui o sovrapposti vicendevolmente
individuo e parola sussistono come soggetti separati:
non un reciproco accordo di parole e di cose
ma il gusto della manomissione.

Le cose esistono per essere dette
e la lingua racconta. Oltraggia a sua volta
in un linguaggio già violato da altri
avere il linguaggio è un modo di essere.

Il soggetto è dunque il linguaggio
con cui perpetrare una personale violazione.

da: SOSTITUZIONE (1973)

POSITIVE & NEGATIVE

Anything may happen
have a meaning or not have one.

It does not propose truth
it keeps the meaning open
the sense of things comes by speaking.

The measure of a page
a communication of forms
the hypothesis of a reality in motion:
a vertigo of infinite
diverse inversions.

And that which is opposed
may be always overturned
to its opposite.

THE SUBJECT IS THE LANGUAGE

An idea of vengeance: the retaliation
or revenge of the word which has been thought
(make the gesture of inventing language
perform the act by which you appropriate language).

Though dependent or superimposed
the individual and the word exist as separate objects:
not a mutual agreement of words and things
but the pleasure of interfering.

Things exist to be said
and language narrates. It outrages in turn
a language already violated by others
to possess language is a way of being.

The subject is therefore the language
with which to commit a capital offense.

    from: SUBSTITUTION (1973)

UTAH

    to Gianfranco Baruchello

Strawberry strawberry
holden monroe
bountiful farmington
minnie plateau.
Emory upton
on devils slide
washington terrace
oh enterprise!
Riverton vernon
elmo woodside
strawberry strawberry
lofgreen lakeside.

REUNION

    to Tiziano

Maria Theresopiel flint Clermont-Ferrand.
Fly Maria, fly.
Forlí John O'Groats (raddom fother-in-ghay)
wiggan soufrière belle belaire:
Levallois Peret (her frischess haff).
Cherry valley Maria, cherry valley.
Yarkhand, yarmouth, rinslip Maria
richfield, richland, richmond.
Loyalty islands lynn Maria.
Merton and morden avenches dee Maria
(lofooten in low countries, lower saxony and new
    guinea).
Hopewell Maria, hopewell.
Virgin isles vaal Maria.
Justice holt Maria.

RISING STAR

Home sweet home sugar land
richland
dripping springs of sweet water
golden acres where sudan

glen rose a sunray
cross plain and blooming grove.
Laredo!
May the crystal sterling silver rising star
fall on dallastexas.

COMO È TRIESTE VENEZIA

    a Charles Aznavour e Adriano Spatola

Igea travagliato
trento treviso e trieste
di disgrazia in disgrazia
fino pomezia.
Como è trieste Venezia . . .

    from: GREENWICH (1971)

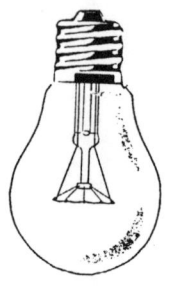

POEMA & OGGETTO

Giulia Niccolai defines the moment in which the mind receives the stimuli of external objects and discovers that these objects have deep and intriguing reverberations inside the self... the analogy between poetry and the moment of childhood which opens to knowledge as it has been handed down by tradition: the moment in which one learns to read... One has the contemporary discovery, and the identification between the lexicon and the language, between the syntax and the narrative unity...

—*Milli Graffi*

[*at left:* THE FOUR PHASES OF THE MOON]

E. V. BALLAD

(a Emilio Villa)

*Ev*ening and the *ev*erest
ist vers la poetry leaning. Er
isst er rit er tells a tale
des bear's der splash! mit cul poilu
nell'acqua bassa um la forelle
zu farla saltar fuori
to make the trout jump out.
Puis il se léve la trota nella paw
und isst und rit und ist der dichter
*ev*ery very big indeed
so froh und bär so rare und weiter.
Ça au national park.
But all america la calzi
come un guanto
zeus rabelais
il t'amusait ce luna-park
you fed computers coded data
coddled eggs cod-fish balls
un cassoulet la fricassée
un potage dame edmée des côtes
de proc grand-mère les couilles
du père and out came *brunt*
H ah quel frisson quel high-toned test
quel high-speed text
tapioca! un bel incest
er mejo the best.
Off frisco *uper the bay*
when rose fingere'd dawn
shone forth that day
nach dem orkan dem hurrican
su quella piramide di phoques
(es war *phil hip* that west coast mentor
qui me l'a dit)
you saw nausicaa and like a mountain lion
dal fitto groviglio dei rami
you broke a spray
athena auch war da she touched your hair
in a certain way
shed grace

and combed it col pettinino azzurro.
Ma sul canto sesto there's nothing more
to say.
Ich wollte ganza for *ever*
once and for all
à la manière de *ev*
von *ev* erzählen et
sinon la *v* qui est si
véri table eventuell
evidenziar la *e*.

        (Febbraio 1975)

A. S. BALLAD

    (a Adriano Spatola)

As ballads go the
A. S. ballad should
soll be
et c'est-à-dire
dovrebbe essere
paramount
tantamount excessive
elle devrait go to extremes
bulge at the seams
schmeck of scotch
and taste of schnaps
donc
elle devrait être
gargantuesque et gongorique
hic
sunt leones
hic et nunc
dovrebbe grow a mane
and wear a beard
und hervorragen
gegen bad poetry klagen
être oversized intemperate
et ressembler enrico ottavo
tuo avo

(sembri fatto in rilievo come
un frutto del crivelli e sono
bianche di marzapane le tue mani
due crespi di banane)
wie er appears in holbein.
Sie soll auch lang sein
and be all mine
(five kilos of macaroni)
farina del mio sacco
full di fatti e di personaggi
difatti le poulet de bresse
alias the breast of chicken
et laszlo katzonis
born in cyprus like othello
ah che bello
e dire di tutto
tutto d'un fiato
e uscire a puntate
come una ballata d'appendice
e cosí via e cosí sia
e sarà fatto.

        (Maggio 1975)

THE LOCKHEED BALLAD

Il "subconscio" del cervello elettronico che aveva fornito ai dirigenti della Lockheed il nome in codice di quei vocaboli, verbi, sigle ecc. che essi non volevano per nessuna ragione essere scoperti a scrivere o pronunciare, aveva, come è giusto, un debole per i grandi personaggi del teatro tragico, in particolare quello shakespeariano. Nel "libretto nero" della Lockheed (supplemento a *Panorama*, 15 giugno 1976) si possono infatti ritrovare: Otello, Desdemona, Cesare, Amleto, Porzia e molti altri. Da parte sua e a suo tempo, Shakespeare si era invece servito di *Rumour* (che in inglese vuol dire chiacchiera, diceria, far correre voce, spargere la voce, vociferare) e che nell'*Enrico IV* (di cui riportiamo l'inizio del prologo della seconda parte) ha il ruolo di presentatore:

INDUCTION

Enter Rumour, *painted full of tongues*
Rum. *Open your ears; for which of you will stop*
The vent of hearing when loud Rumour speaks?
. . .

(Penso che il lettore abbia modo di consultare il seguito che vale la pena di essere riletto in questa chiave). In prospettiva struttuale, esaminando ulteriormente i vocaboli cifrati del "libretto nero", ci rendiamo conto di poterli suddividere in altre tre grandi categorie: nomi tratti dalla flora e dalla fauna (antilope, lillà, leone, iris ecc.), nomi che hanno connotazioni eroico-epiche (argonauta, cosmo, gladiatore ecc.) e parole tipicamente sassoni, monosillabiche e onomatopeiche che corrispondono a volte ai "rumori scritti" dei fumetti americani, come ad esempio: *sob* (che in inglese vuol dire piangere, singhiozzare), *jab* (accoltellare), *tap* (bussare alla porta) ecc.
Data la ricchezza del materiale presente nel "libretto nero" della Lockheed, è chiaro che si possono ottenere un numero infinito di testi poetici o teatrali (epici, tragici, comici ecc.)

THE LOCKHEED BALLAD

The electronic brain's "subconscious" that had
furnished Lockheed's executives with code names
for those terms, words, initials, etc, which they
under no circumstances wanted to be discovered
writing or uttering, had, as it should, a weakness
for the great characters of tragic drama, particularly
Shakespearean. In Lockheed's "little black book"
(supplement to *Panorama,* June 15, 1976) we can
in fact discover: Othello, Desdemona, Caesar,
Hamlet, Portia and many others.
For his part and time, Shakespeare instead
employed *Rumour* (which in English means
chatter, talk, spreading stories, not holding one's
tongue, gossip-mongering) and which in *Henry IV*
(here we cite the opening of the prologue to part two)
has the role of announcer:

INDUCTION

Enter Rumour, *painted full of tongues*
Rum. Open your ears; for which of you will stop
The vent of hearing when loud Rumour speaks?
. . . .

(I think the reader might consult the
following as worth rereading in this
light). From a structural perspective, further
examining the coded terms in the "little black book",
we realize they may be subdivided into three other
broad categories: names taken from flora and fauna
(antelope, lilac, lion, iris, etc), names with
heroic-epic connotations,(argonaut, cosmos,
gladiator, etc) and words typically Anglo-Saxon,
monosyllabic and onomatopoeic which sometimes
correspond to the "written sounds" of American comics,
such as: *sob* (which in English means to cry, to make
a weeping sound), *jab* (to knife), *tap* (to knock on
the door), etc.
Given the richness of the material present in
Lockheed's "little black book", it's clear
we might obtain an infinite number of poetic
or theatrical texts (epic, tragic, comic, etc)

e che questi testi, con la traduzione simultanea
del vocabolo criptico nel suo significato reale
(o viceversa) offrono innumerevoli possibilità
di giochi di parole a due o piú voci come in una
specie di battaglia navale verbale. Ma per
classificare e elaborare in tutte le loro possibili
combinazioni i vocaboli del "libretto nero" è
ovviamente indispensabile un altro cervello
elettronico. Il testo che ho scelto di scrivere
è composto esclusivamente di parole tratte
(nella loro accezione cifrata) dal "libretto nero",
si serve dei nomi di personaggi shakespeariani
ivi presenti e può essere letto come ballata o
come epilogo a un ibrido innesto di tragedie
e commedie.

Othello's feline ire forbs his granite
Fingers; his vim hath sealed his willow
Goddess' lips. The flametree's firethorn
Doth spear the Lady's reb; Desdemona
The jonquil, the ladybird, the opal oriole
Now cold and dab like flotsam upon
The tidal ebb. Woe to Hamlet, the moonbeam
Upon his silver sword, the bleak phantom's vox,
The prophet's raven cloak, the hemlock
And the hammer hard. An ode to Juliet
To Portia, to the actors in the barnyard.

(Settembre 1976)

and that these texts, with a simultaneous translation
of the cryptic vocabulary into its actual meaning
(or viceversa) offer innumerable possibilities
of wordplay in two or more voices as in a sort
of naval battle of words. But to classify and
elaborate the terms in the "little black book"
in all their possible combinations
another electronic brain is clearly
indispensable. The text I've chosen to write
is composed exclusively of words taken
(in their coded meaning) from the "little black book";
it uses the names of Shakespearean characters
there present and may be read as a ballad or
an epilogue to a hybrid of tragedies
and comedies.

Othello's feline ire forbs his granite
Fingers; his vim hath sealed his willow
Goddess' lips. The flametree's firethorn
Doth spear the Lady's reb; Desdemona
The jonquil, the ladybird, the opal oriole
Now cold and dab like flotsam upon
The tidal ebb. Woe to Hamlet, the moonbeam
Upon his silver sword, the black phantom's vox,
The prophet's raven cloak, the hemlock
And the hammer hard. An ode to Juliet
To Portia, to the actors in the barnyard.

(September 1976)

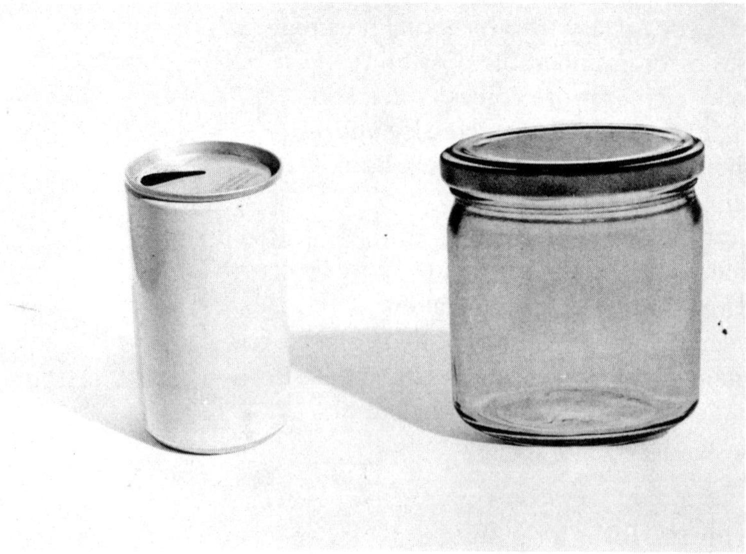

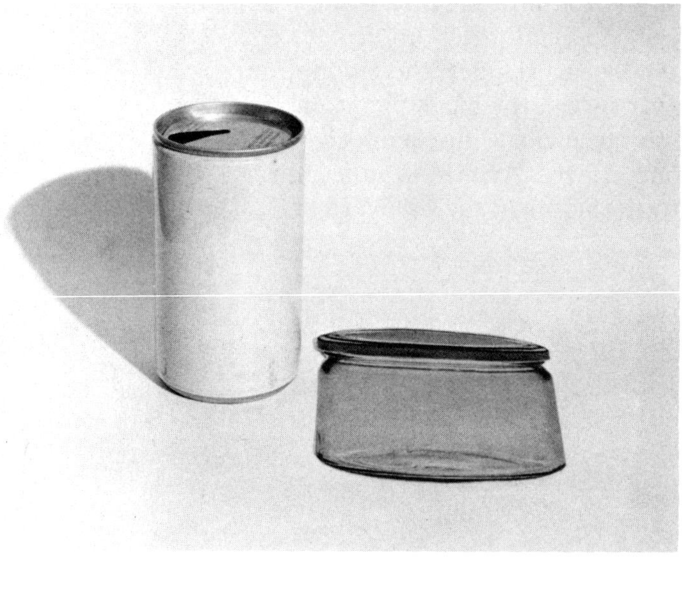

I

The photograph of a metal beer can and of a jar cut out of a magazine. If one photographs the two objects in the same identical perspective in which the glass has been photographed beforehand, one will obtain a beer can which is as misshapen as the jar and the jar, even if it is being photographed for the second time, will not undergo any further transformations of shape.

II

We can say at this point that, once photographed, an object transforms itself into a photographed subject and thus remains.

III

One could therefore photograph, cut out of the printed photograph and photograph again and again an infinite number of times the jar, put next to the metal can (let us say) the twentyfifth photograph of the jar, and one will always obtain the same result. *As long as one goes on photographing in the original perspective.* (which is not the case of this sequence)

[1977]

POET-PUBLIC, PUBLIC-POET

(Poet raises left arm).
"To the right is my right hand. But for me it's my left hand. Right?"

(Poet raises right arm).
"To the left is my left hand. But for me it's my right hand. Right?
What is right and what is left?
Both you and I are left with two hands.
The problem is to see whether it's better to speak about these hands from your point of view or from mine — which is exactly opposite".

"If I were left-handed, would I put my pen in my left hand to write?
I would put it in my right hand to show you that I am left-handed".
(Poet puts pen in right hand).

"And if I were writing in the air, would I write from left to right or from right to left?
I would write from right to left".
(Poet writes in the air from right to left).

"Two positives in a mirror don't make a negative.
I appear to be positively left-handed.
If all of you now maintain that I am left-handed and I maintain I'm not, would your word be better than mine?"
(Poet counts people in the public).
"The ratio is about...to one.
Would I have a chance?"
"I now cross my arms".
(Poet crosses raised arms to make an 'X').
"Right is now right for you and left for me.
Left is left to you and right for me.
I cannot write with my hands in this position, but I *have* written.
Have I written the Roman number 'ten' or an 'X'?"

"The Roman number 'ten' is an 'X' made up by two
    'V's one upside down, the other upside up
The 'V' is the Roman number 'five'.
Five and five make ten".
(Poet makes 'V' sign with index and middle fingers).
"But the 'V' also means 'two'.
The 'V' also means 'Victory'.
I now cancel everything with the 'X' and try to add
    two hands, a victory, the numbers 2, 5 and 10".
(Poet mumbles as if adding up).
"I subtract all of these from all of you.
Whatever is left can't be anything but right".

(Amsterdam, October 1979)

(photo by Christophe Schimmel)

FRISBEES

> *a Bob McB,*
> *messaggero degli dei di Cazadero Valley*

Una volta
aprendo il frigorifero
è capitato anche a me di dire:
"C'è qualcosa di marcio in Danimarca".

IS mi dice di aver visto vicino a Porta Romana
un picolou ristouranti Thaigliandeisi.
"Ma, come", dico io, "il ristorante si chiama Italian Daisy?"
"Ma, come", dice lui, "Italian Daisy? Thaigliandeisi".
"Ah, Thailandese!", dico io.
(Lui, IS, mi stava parlando in italiano
e io lo stavo ascoltando in inglese).
E pensare che la più "bella" signora dell'orto
che io ero convinta si chiamasse Italia,
si chiama invece Margherita.

Non si gioca a *Frisbee* solo con le parole.
È bene farlo anche con le braccia e con le gambe.

"Beati i poveri di spirito"
dovrebbe fare in inglese:
"Blessed are the half-wits".
Invece è: "Blessed are the poor in spirit".
(Anche per questo bevo sempre parecchio).

I Presidenti degli Stati Uniti
(da quando televisione è televisione)
e quando parlano al popolo americano,
fissano sempre un punto sopra l'obiettivo della camera.
(Vedi: orizzonte. Vedi: infinito).
Ma, ce li hanno i piedi per terra?

Attenta che i *Frisbees*
possono diventare nauseanti.
È importante l'ordine in cui si susseguono.

FRISBEES

>   *for Bob McB,*
>   *messenger of the gods of Cazadero Valley*

Once
opening the refrigerator
I too happened to say:
"There's something rotten in the state of Denmark".

IS tells me he saw near Porta Romana
a littel restourant Thaigliandeisi.
"What", I say, "the restaurant is called Italian Daisy?"
"What", he says, "Italian Daisy? Thaigliandeisi".
"Ah, Thailandese!", I say.
(He, IS, was speaking to me in Italian
and I was listening to him in English).
To think that the "fairest" lady in the garden
whom I was convinced is called Italia,
is called instead Margherita.

One doesn't play *Frisbee* only with words.
It's good to do it also with arms and legs.

"Beati i poveri di spirito"
ought to come out in English:
"Blessed are the half-wits".
Instead it's: "Blessed are the poor in spirit".
(Because of this too I drink a lot).

Presidents of the United States
(from when television is television)
and when they speak to the American people,
always fix on a spot above the camera lens.
(See: horizon. See: infinite).
But do they have their feet on the ground?

Careful that the *Frisbees*
may become nauseating.
The order in which they follow each other is important.

Certo che può esserci qualcosa
che ancora sfugge
sia a me che a voi
in tutto questo!
Sto diventando una poetessa impegnata.
Sto diventando una poetessa impegnata?

Poter constatare
la mattina dopo,
serenamente,
alla luce del giorno
che anche la propria presunzione
e stupidità
non hanno fondo,
non hanno limite
. . .
è una cosa bellissima.

Consiglio l'ascolto di Bach
agli artritici e ai reumatici.
Al contrario del freddo,
dell'umido
— e come gli ultrasuoni —
cura
quando ti entra nelle ossa.
Holy Bach heals.
Holy Bach makes whole. Perbacco!

(Rilassarsi
in modo da ascoltarne le vibrazioni
anche con le ossa).

Pensiamo al cervello
come a una prugna secca.
Immergiamolo in Bach.
Si gonfia e pulsa
come una spugna.

Bach è bello averlo nel sangue.

Certainly there may be something
still elusive
in all this
be it for me or you!
I am becoming a committed poetess.
I am becoming a committed poetess?

To be able to establish
the morning after,
serenely,
in the light of day
that even my own presumption
and stupidity
are bottomless,
are limitless . . .
. . .
is a most lovely thing.

I suggest listening to Bach
for arthritics and rheumatics.
Opposite of cold,
of humidity
— and like ultrasonics —
it heals
as it enters your bones.
Holy Bach heals.
Holy Bach makes whole. By Jove!

(Relax
so as to hear the vibrations
even with the bones).

Let's think of the brain
as a shrivelled prune.
Immerse it in Bach.
It swells and pulses
like a sponge.

Bach is beautiful to have in the blood.

L'organista e clavicembalista
che suona Johann Sebastian
si chiama Janos Sebestyen.
Cos'altro poteva fare?

Mi sono fatta
una maschera facciale
con la *Toccata concertata*
(in mi maggiore BWV 566)
di Bach.

Il modo in cui cammino
mi ha sempre fatto consumare
il lato esterno dei tacchi delle scarpe.
Giocando a *Frisbee*
vorrei cominciare a consumare un po'
anche quello interno.
Per equilibrare.
Vorrei anche che i *Frisbees*
mi aiutassero
a far funzionare il cervello
in modo nuovo.
Chiedo troppo?
A questo scopo
potrebbe essere utile
cominciare a chiamarli
Frisbeezen o *Zen-frisbees*.

E questo cos'è?
Un *Frisbee* di testa o di gambe?

E perché non ho scritto
un *Frisbee* di gambe o di testa?

(I primi passi
sono sempre un po' problematici).

What about a *Porno-frisbee?*
Yeah. A dirty-minded one.

The organist and the clavichordist
who plays Johann Sebastian
is called Janos Sebestyen.
What else could he do?

I gave myself
a facial
with the *Orchestral Toccata*
(in E major BWV 566)
of Bach.

The way I walk
has always made me wear down
the outside edge of the heels of my shoes.
Playing *Frisbee*
I wish to begin wearing down a little
the inside one also.
For equilibrium.
I wish also the *Frisbees*
might help me
make my mind work
a new way.
Do I ask too much?
For this purpose
it might help
to start calling them
Frisbeezen or *Zen-frisbees*.

So what's this?
A *Frisbee* of head or legs?

And why didn't I write
a *Frisbee* of legs or head?

(The first steps
are always a little problematic).

What about a *Porno-frisbee?*
Yeah. A dirty-minded one.

Comunque
(e qui andiamo sul liscio),
i *Frisbeezen*
suonano più tedeschi
dei *Zen-frisbees*
che a loro volta
suonano più californiani
che giapponesi.
(Siamo sempre molto lontani dal satori).

Chiede IS passando per Piazza Sempione:
"Ma questo si chiama
Arco della Pace o
Arco di Trionfo?"
"Trionfo a Parigi, Pace a Milano".

Quando ieri ho scritto
che mi sono fatta
una maschera facciale
con la *Toccata concertata*
intendevo dire
che la *Toccata concertata*
— mentre veniva toccata e concertata —
mi scioglieva sul volto,
mi spianava
i grumi di ansia e di paura.

Una delle ragioni per cui
da ragazza ho fatto la fotografa
è anche quella
di essere sempre dietro la macchina fotografica
e mai davanti.
(Infantti, chi fotografa
non viene quasi mai fotografato).
Non allo specchio
ma nelle fotografie che mi ritraevano
distinguevo la paura sul mio volto.

Anna dà un'occhiata
alla prima cartella di *Frisbees*
e mi chiede:
"Sono tutti sul cibo?"
"Minestrone, minestrone", le rispondo.

In any case
(and here we're on easy ground),
the *Frisbeezen*
sound more German
than *Zen-frisbees*
which in turn
sound more Californian
than Japanese.
(We're still a long way from *satori*).

IS asks passing through Piazza Sempione:
"Is this called
Arch of Peace or
Arch of Triumph?"
"Triumph in Paris, Peace in Milano".

When I wrote yesterday
that I gave myself
a facial
with the *Orchestral Toccata*
I meant to say
that the *Orchestral Toccata*
— while being toccata and orchestrated —
dissolved on my face,
smoothed away
the lumps of anxiety and fear.

One of the reasons why
as a girl I was a photographer
is also that
of being always behind the camera
never in front.
(In fact, who photographs
is almost never photographed).
Not in the mirror
but in the photographs that caught me
I made out the fear on my face.

Anna glances
at the first page of the *Frisbees*
and asks me:
"Are they all about food?"
"Minestrone, minestrone", I answer.

G.G.F. fired one of his editors
with a gun in his hand.
Evidently G.G.F.
was thinking in English
while he was doing it...

Ho due portacenere
a forma di cuore.
Lo so che fumo troppo.
Mi farò cremare.

Coltivare il linguaggio come l'orto.
Coltivare l'orto come il linguaggio.
Raccogliere i pistelli e le taccole
mi ricorda la correzione della bozze.
Come gli errori
non si riesce mai a individuarli tutti.
Per svista ne rimangono sempre un paio sulla pianta.

Evidentemente
ma
a mia insputa,
sto cominciando a praticare
la scrittura automatica surrealista
oppure
la scrittura automatica surrealista
sta cominciando a praticare me.
Vedi il *Frisbee* della maschera facciale
che segue quello su Janos.
Giano. Giano Bifronte.

Non vorrei che i *Frisbees*
fossero il mio testamento.
Certo, però, hanno qualcosa
del cadavre exquis.

Chiamavo mio padre affettuosamente "Rinoceronte",
"Rinoceronte ingiallito".
Anni dopo la sua morte
ho sognato un rinoceronte
che, con il lungo corno,
annusava un papavero in un campo.

G.G.F. fired one of his editors
with a gun in his hand.
Evidently G.G.F.
was thinking in English
while he was doing it . . .

I have two ashtrays
in the shape of a heart.
I know I smoke too much.
I shall have myself cremated.

To cultivate language like a garden.
To cultivate a garden like language.
Picking beans and peas
reminds me of correcting proof.
How one never manages
to single out all the mistakes.
Through oversight a couple always remain on the plant.

Evidently
but
unknown to me,
I am beginning to practice
surrealist automatic writing
or surrealist automatic writing
is beginning to practice me.
See the *Frisbee* about the facial
that follows the one on Janos.
Janus. Two-faced Janus.

I wouldn't want the *Frisbees*
to be my testament.
Certainly, though, they have something
of the exquisite corpse about them.

I called my father affectionately "Rhinoceros",
"old yellow Rhinoceros".
Years after his death
I dreamt of a rhinoceros
sniffing with his horn
at a poppy in a field.

E si infuriava,
si imbestialiva
e si incazzava
perché con il corno (otturato)
non era in grado di sentirne il profumo.
(Io, nel sogno sapevo
che i papaveri non hanno odore
ma non osavo avvicinarmi al rinoceronte
per dirglielo).
Il rinoceronte da lontano
si dimenava e scalciava.
Poi, per rabbia, per spregio,
pisciò sul papavero.
Ci fece sopra una lunga, poderosa pisciata.
PAPAVERO.
PAPÀ VERO.
Ciao, Sigmund!

Food for thought.
We do not teach
And we are not taught.
And we are not taut.

Roman Polanski.
E abbiamo un Papa Roman Polanski.
È stato Paul Vangelisti
di Los Angeles
a farmi capire
che polacchi e italiani si assomigliano.
Petrus, dove sei?
Mi sei mancato alla *Pasticceria*.
Fanno un'ottima Torta Paradiso,
ça va sans dire.

Stampati
i *Frisbees*
andrebbero
tanto distanziati
da permettere
a chi lo vuole
8358618
di scrivere i propri
negli spazi bianchi.

And he got furious
he got beastly
and pissed off
because with his horn (plugged up)
he couldn't smell the perfume.
(I knew, in the dream,
that poppies have no smell
but I didn't dare get near the rhinoceros
to tell him).
The rhinoceros in the distance
fussed and stamped.
Then, in anger, with contempt,
he pissed on the poppy.
He let go on top of it a long, mighty piss.
POPPY
POP PEE
Ciao, Sigmund!

Food for thought.
We do not teach
And we are not taught.
And we are not taut.

Roman Polanski.
Now we have a Roman Polanski Pope.
It was Paul Vangelisti
of Los Angeles
who made me understand
that Poles and Italians resemble each other.
Petrus, where are you?
I missed you at the *Pasticceria.*
They make an excellent Paradise Tort,
ça va sans dire.

Printed
the *Frisbees*
should be
so spread apart
to permit
whoever wants
8358618
to write their own
in the empty spaces.

L'8358618
si trova
in brutta
lì dove ora
si trova qui
in bella.

Vista l'altra sera
dietro le quinte
a San Maurizio
dopo un concerto di Bach:
la custodia di un violoncello
usata come gruccia
per una giacca da uomo.
Caro Many Ray, era tua la giacca drappeggiata sulla custodia come
su un manichino? L'avevi messa lì mentre suonavi il Violon d'Ingres?

Scritto il *Frisbee*
mi prende la voglia di consultare
Man Ray Fotografo (Idea Books)
e appena lo apro
l'occhio mi cade sul nome di
Manrico Nicolai
Assessore di Pietrasanta
che firma una breve introduzione al libro.

Credo che la magia
ci sfiori in continuazione.
È colpa nostra
se non la riconosciamo.
Se non l'apprezziamo.

Caro Giorgio,
Caro Diòloch,
could a *Freeze*
be
frozen words in space
which want to fly?
Or a *bee* looking for honey?
O un'amletica *be*?

The 8358618
is found
in rough copy
there where now
is found
in fair.

Seen the other night
in the wings
at San Maurizio
after a Bach concert:
a cello case
used as a hanger
for a man's coat.
Dear Man Ray, was that your coat draped on the case as
on a dummy? Did you put it there while playing Ingres' Violon?

That *Frisbee* written
I feel the urge to consult
Man Ray Photographer (Idea Books)
and soon as I open it
my eye lights on the name
Manrico Nicolai
Commissioner of Pietrasanta
author of the brief introduction.

I think magic
brushes against us continually.
It's our fault
if we don't recognize it.
If we don't understand it.

Dear Giorgio,
Dear Dioloch,
could a Freeze
be
frozen words in space
which want to fly?
Or a *bee* looking for honey?
Or an Hamletic *be*?

Il *Goethe-Frisbee*.
C'era sul davanzale
una lattina di birra *Oranjeboom*.
Lattina nera che noto
guardando fuori dalla finestra
quando anche l'asfalto
è nero di pioggia.
Dico: "Quanto si assomigliano
e che belli che sono
il nero della lattina
il nero dell'asfalto".
Poi noto la piantina d'arancio
e registro
gli Orange reali d'Olanda.
Poi però
(e qui non so se sia colpa
di Marguerite Yourcenar
che sto leggendo
e che in *Les yeux ouverts*
parla di Goethe),
di colpo mi viene in mente
questo verso demente:
"Kennst du das Land wo die Oranjeboom".

Frisbees now
give me a high.
Do I know
why do you know
why?

A Paola Rossi.
Baudelaire e Rimbaud
hanno *baud* in comune.
Rimbaud, rainbow
e dunque anche
i colori delle vocali.

Sempre sul fumo.
I know two people
who fume more than I do:
Joan Arnold and
Adriano Spatola.

The *Goethe-Frisbee*.
There was on the windowsill
a can of *Oranjeboom* beer.
Black can I notice
looking out the window
when the asphalt too
is black with rain.
I say: "How much alike
and how beautiful they are
the black of the can
the black of the asphalt".
Then I notice the little orange tree
and register
the Dutch House of Orange.
But then
(and here I'm not sure if it isn't the fault
of Marguerite Yourcenar
whom I'm reading
and who in *Les yeux ouverts*
speaks of Goethe),
suddenly this demented line
springs to mind:
"Kennst du das Land wo die Oranjeboom".

Frisbees now
give me a high.
Do I know
why do you know
why?

For Paola Rossi.
Baudelaire and Rimbaud
have *baud* in common.
Rimbaud, rainbow
and so too
the colors of vowels.

Still on smoking.
I know two people
who fume more than I do:
Joan Arnold and
Adriano Spatola.

Paul called a third time
from Los Angeles
at midnight
— was it yesterday or today?
to find out Goofy's name in Italian.
It's Pippo.

In *Auto da fé*
scritto nel '35
Elias Canetti
crea Fischerle
un nano
giocatore di scacchi
che sogna di andare in America
battere Capablanca
e chiamarsi Fischer.
Tiens, tiens: Bobby Fischer!

Elias Canetti
nelle foto del Nobel
ha i capelli bianchi.
Tiens, tiens: Capablanca!

Ho due settimane di *Frisbees*
scritti un po' da tutte le parti
e non ancora ribattuti.
Ne ho sull'agenda, dietro le buste
di lettere che mi sono arrivate,
su tovaglioli di carta.
Questi ultimi
li ho ricopiati
dal piano di marmo
del tavolo di cucina.
Scritti a matita
come i conti
dei macellai d'antan.

Chiedo di pagare due rossi
al cassiere delle *Scimmie*.
"Vino?" mi chiede lui.
(Deve essere molto politicizzato).

Paul called a third time
from Los Angeles
at midnight
— was it yesterday or today? —
to find out Goofy's name in Italian.
It's Pippo.

In *Auto da fè*
written in 1935
Elias Canetti
creates Fischerle
a dwarf
chess player
who dreams of going to America
beating Capablanca
and calling himself Fischer.
Tiens, tiens: Bobby Fischer!

Elias Canetti
in the Nobel photo
has white hair.
Tiens, tiens: Capablanca!

I have two weeks of *Frisbees*
scribbled here and there
and not yet typed out.
I have some in my notebook, on the backs of envelopes
of letters I've gotten,
on paper napkins.
These last
I've recopied
from the marble top
of the kitchen table.
Written in pencil
like the sums
of the butchers d'antan.

I tell the cashier at the *Scimmie*
I want to pay for two reds.
"Wine?" he asks me.
(He must be very politicized).

Dopo poco al bar
vedo il sosia di Pavese
e il sosia di Sanguineti.
Saranno mica questi allora
i due rossi del cassiere?

E io
quante ore dovrei rimanere al bar
quanti rossi dovrei bere
prima di vedere
la sosia di me stessa?

A volte
uso lo specchietto della borsa
come portacenere.

Oh come odora
come profuma di uova e sale
quel sentore
che da sotto le lenzuola sale.
Caviale!

Corrado mi dice
di avere la casa piena
di vasetti di miele *pieni*.
Non da mangiare.
Solo da guardare.

(Ma tu guarda!
Il sesso!
Che razza di libertà si prende!
Che trasformismi!)

I know now no no now I know
no no *now* I know
who National Velvet is
who National Velvet really was
what National Velvet
must have stood for. Cazzo!

Soon after at the bar
I see Pavese's double
and Sanguineti's double.
Could these be then
the cashier's two reds?

And I
how many hours must I stay at the bar
how many reds must I drink
before I see
my own double?

Sometimes
I use my pocket mirror
as an ashtray.

O how it smells
how it perfumes of eggs and salt
that scent
that from under the sheet rises.
Caviar!

Corrado tells me
he keeps a house full
of *full* honey pots.
Not to eat.
Just to look at.

(But look!
Sex!
What liberties it takes!
What transformations!)

I know now no no now I know
no no *now* I know
who National Velvet is
who National Velvet really was
what National Velvet
must have stood for. Cazzo!

As nice and as (up)right
as a spoon
spooning in a pot of honey.
As a spoon
spooning in a lake of honey.

Per spiegare alle sue amiche
americane e inglesi
quanto poco sapesse l'italiano,
mia madre era solita dire:
"I give *tu* to strangers
and *lei* my husband".

Non ho mai capito
se capisse quello che diceva.
Ma forse risale al fatto di aver capito
il doppiosenso di quel *lei*
il mio giocare con le parola.

Sono nata il 21-12-'34
21 e 12 sono anagrammati
e poi abbiamo anche 1,2,3,4.
Potrebbe essere elegante
morire a 56 anni
per poter fare 1,2,3,4,5,6.
Avrò 56 anni nel '90.
Il 1991 però andrebbe meglio.
Farebbe da pendant al 21-12.
In questo caso sarei favorevole
a una lapide così concepita:
Nata il 21-12-1934
Morta il 3-4-1991.
Difficile scegliere tra i 56 anni
e il 1991.
Ma Giulia,
non si può avere tutto dalla vita!

When I'll want to embrace you
and you'll happen not to be around...
I'll start washing
your heavy, large, English woollen cardigan.
I'll get into the tub with it.

As nice and as (up)right
as a spoon
spooning in a pot of honey.
As a spoon
spooning in a lake of honey.

To explain to her woman friends
American and English
how little she knew Italian,
my mother would always say:
"I give *tu* to strangers
and *lei* my husband".

I have never understood
whether she realized what she was saying.
But perhaps my playing with words
comes from having understood
the double meaning of that *lei*.

I was born 12-21-34.
12 and 21 are anagrammatic
and then we have 1,2,3,4.
It would be elegant
to die at 56
to be able to make 1,2,3,4,5,6.
I'll be 56 in '90.
1991 though would be better.
It would make a pair with 12-21.
In this case I'd favor
a stone planned thus:
Born 12-21-1934
Died 3-4-1991.
Hard to choose between age 56
and 1991.
But Giulia,
we can't have everything in life.

When I'll want to embrace you
and you'll happen not to be around...
I'll start washing
your large, heavy, English woollen cardigan.
I'll get into the tub with it.

Il marito di Margherita — alias Italia —
(che prima d'ora non avevo mai visto all'orto),
appena veniamo presentati mi dice:
"Ma lei veste come una thailandese!"
Questa ormai è pura magia.

A proposito di National Velvet.
Il manifesto delle linee aeree thailandesi
appeso nel ristorante thailandese
vicino a Porta Romana dice:
"As smooth as silk
Now in Jumbo size".
Erotismo orientale?

Forse anche Geppetto
sapeva l'inglese.
Comunque,
lo si può leggere
anche così:
the wood is the would.

È molto importante vedere
Il fascino discreto della borghesia
prima di cena. A stomaco vuoto.

Si potrebbero lanciare Frisbees per l'eternità
e si farebbero aureole
                      aureole
                                aureole.

Un *Frisbee* spontaneo
che si è auto-costruito
mentre lo dicevo a Marcello Angioni
senza nemmeno averlo pensato:
"Il quadro è
la chiesa di Sant'Agostino
vista da Della Casa
dalla sua casa
in via Sant'Agostino 33".
(Dunque, il quadro
di Giuliano è un *Frisbee*).
Spazio e tempo, olé!

The husband of Margherita — alias Italia —
(whom before now I'd never seen in the garden),
soon as we are introduced tells me:
"But you dress like a thailandese!"
This by now is pure magic.

Apropos National Velvet.
A poster for Thailand Airlines
hanging in the Thai restaurant
near Porta Romana says:
"As smooth as silk
Now in Jumbo size"
Oriental eroticism?

Perhaps even Geppetto
knew English.
Anyhow,
it can be read
like this:
the wood is the would.

It's very important to see
The Discreet Charm of the Bourgeoisie
before dinner. On an empty stomach.

We could throw Frisbees eternally
and they would make haloes
                        haloes
                                haloes.

A spontaneous *Frisbee*
that composed itself
as I spoke to Marcello Angioni
not even having thought about it:
The painting is
the church of Sant'Agostino
seen by Della Casa
from his house
in via Sant'Agostino 33".
(Thus, Giuliano's
painting is a *Frisbee*).
Space and time, olè!

Shame is a horse
who rides
who likes it.

Giuseppe e Maria
sono *anche*
l'esatto contrario
di Adamo ed Eva?

A Modena
l'amico di un amico
a cui leggo un paio di *Frisbees*
dice: "Sono molto Snoopy".
È vero. È vero.
E mi va anche bene.
Perché allora ci rimango male?
Perché l'ha detto come lo direbbe Lucy.

Titolo di *La Repubblica*
7 dicembre 1982:
"Ustinov a Reagan: 'Non ci batterete'".
Cinema batte realtà 2 a O.

It wasn't
to be or not to be.
It was to be but I forgot.

Two koalas on a tree
make three koalas
or the koalas' tree.

Spike spoke: "Umbrella".

Even writing *lies* on the page.

Nei politici
la meschinità
è raramente

Shame is a horse
who rides
who likes it.

Joseph and Mary
are *also*
the exact opposite
of Adam and Eve?

In Modena
a friend of a friend
to whom I read a couple of *Frisbees*
says: "They're very Snoopy".
Which is perfectly true
and suits me fine.
Why then do I take it badly?
Because he said it as Lucy would.

Headline in *La Repubblica*
December 7, 1982:
"Ustinov to Reagan: 'You won't beat us'".
Cinema beats reality 2-0.

It wasn't
to be or not to be.
It was to be but I forgot.

Two koalas on a tree
make three koalas
or the koalas tree.

Spike spoke: "Umbrella".

Even writing *lies* on the page.

In politicians
pettiness
is rarely

evidente.
Infatti,
cercano il potere
per poter essere
tutto
fuorché meschini.

Essendo la meschinità
la caratteristica
più spontanea
degli uomini.

In writing *Frisbees*
I don't think people
necessarily like
what I say
because they can see
the way
my mind works.
"Thank you, Gertrude".

To spring into Summer
and fall into Winter.

E se le parole fossero angeli custodi?

Il suo braccio nel sonno
appoggiato alla mia vita
è il remo nello scalmo
e il resto è acqua
              acqua
                    acqua.

Ricevo il n. 12 del *Cervo volante*
con una bella poesia di Sanguineti
il cui ultimo verso dice:
"ma adesso che ti ho visto, vita mia, spegnimi gli occhi
    con due dita, e basta:"
e per associazione
mi torna in mente
come, nel '63

evident.
In fact,
they seek power
to have the power to be
anything
but petty.

Pettiness being
the most spontaneous
characteristic
of men.

In writing *Frisbees*
I don't think people
necessarily like
what I say
because they can see
the way my mind works.
"Thank you, Gertrude".

To spring into Summer
and fall into Winter.

And if words were guardian angels?

His arm in sleep
resting on my waist
is the oar in the oarlock
and the rest is water
                    water
                          water.

I receive *Cervo volante 12*
with a beautiful poem of Sanguineti's
the last line of which says:
"but now that I have seen you, my life, shut my eyes with two
    fingers, that's enough:"
and by association
comes to mind
how, in '63

Sanguineti dicesse di sè
(e molti dissero e scrissero di Sanguineti)
che in ogni città d'Italia
c'erano due o tre studenti
disposti a morire per lui.

Gli adulti?!
Una categoria che ho conosciuto solo da bambina.

Car la mort n'est qu'un jeu
comparé à l'amour
                Shakespeare & Piaf

Delle volte
spengo la sigaretta
nella lente d'ingrandimento.

La Madonna di Loreto.
Il pappagello che si chiama *Loreto*.
Mussolini appeso in Piazza Loreto.
Tutto *Made in Italy*.

There is
relatively
little fear
on my part
of being
ridiculous
because
I have always been
ridiculous
in my fear.

La Sfinge ha
non solo il corpo
ma *anche* il collo
da animale.
Altrimenti
non potrebbe tenere
la testa così eretta.
(Provare per crederci).

Sanguineti said of himself
(and many said and wrote it of Sanguineti)
that in every Italian city
there were two or three students
ready to die for him.

Adults?
A category I knew only as a child.

Car la mort n'est qu'un jeu
comparè à l'amour
                    Shakespeare & Piaf

Sometimes
I put out a cigarette
in a magnifying glass.

The Madonna of Loreto.
The parrot named *Loreto*.
Mussolini hung in Piazzo Loreto.
All *Made in Italy*.

There is
relatively
little fear
on my part
of being
ridiculous
because
I have always been
ridiculous
in my fear.

The Sphinx has
not only the body
but the neck too
of an animal.
Otherwise
it couldn't hold
its head so straight.
(Try it to believe it).

Leggendo i *Pensieri diversi*
di Wittgenstein,
molte volte (lo confesso),
ho avuto la tentazione
di leggere per primi
quelli che Wittgenstein ha scritto nel 1934
anno della mia nascita.
Non l'ho fatto.
Ma li ho letti comunque perché ora sono al '47.
Attribuiti al '34
di pensieri ce n'è 4.
E li ho capiti.
Sono nata sotto una stella fortunata?

Secondo Wittgenstein
Shakespeare
è una specie di Gargantua
della lingua.

Sono finita su un *7 Bello* per Roma
e ho avuto la sensazione
che i passeggeri seduti vicino a me
non mi prendessero per una borghese.
È solo invecchiando
che me è venuta
quest'aria da "artista".
Che lezione, mia cara, che lezione!

Ad Alfredo Giuliani.
Il mio peccato capitale
è l'orgoglio.
Lo sconto
(per una coincidenza beffarda
quasi Zen)
non ottendo
mai niente
se chiedo qualcosa.

Se invece
sono gli altri
che chiedono a me
. . .

Reading Wittgenstein's
Vermischte Bemerkungen
many times (I confess),
I had the temptation
to read first
those which Wittgenstein wrote in 1934
the year of my birth.
I didn't do it.
But I read them anyway because now I'm at '47.
Attributed to '34
there are four thoughts.
And I understood them.
Was I born under a lucky star?

According to Wittgenstein
Shakespeare
is a sort of Gargantua
of language.

I ended up on the Super Flyer for Rome
and I had the feeling
the passengers sitting near me
didn't take me for a bourgeoise.
It's only with age
that I've acquired
this air of the "artist".
What a lesson, my dear, what a lesson!

To Alfredo Giuliani.
My capital sin
is pride.
I atone
(by a mocking coincidence
almost Zen)
never obtaining
anything
I ask for.

If, instead
it's others
who ask of me
. . .

tutto va liscio.
Riesco persino a dire di no.

Scritto in stampatello a matita
sulla panchina dei giardinetti
sulla quale sono seduta:
LA CATARSI PURIFICA LO SPIRITO
(PROVACI ANCHE TU).
Mentre sto ricopiando la scritta nell'agenda,
un signore anziano
prima di sedersi
sulla panchina accanto
compie quel gesto ormai dimenticato
di spolverare il sedile
con un fazzoletto bianco immacolato.

Mi piacciono i nonni (pensionati)
a spasso con i nipotini (di un anno e mezzo, due)
nei giardini.
Sono spesso
entrambi
così imbarazzati.
E poiché sono tanto educati
da cercare di nasconderselo
l'un l'altro,
il loro disagio
è visibile
al quadrato.
Soprattutto quando si guardano.
Quando si fermano e si guardano.

Lo confesso
— disse in un sussurro —
non ho letto Saussure.

Comunque il fascino
di Saussure
sta nel fatto
che anche chi l'ha letto
non è in grado di spiegarlo
(a voce) ad altri.

everything goes smoothly.
I even manage to say no.

Lettered in ink
on the bench in the gardens
on which I sit:
CATHARSIS PURIFIES THE SPIRIT
(TRY IT YOURSELF).
While I'm copying this in my notebook,
an elderly man
before he sits down
on the nearby bench
makes that gesture by now forgotten
of dusting the seat
with an immaculate white handkerchief.

I like grandfathers (retired)
strolling with their grandsons (a year-and-a-half, two)
in the gardens.
They are often
both
so embarrassed.
And because they are so well-mannered
as to try to hide it
one from the other,
their discomfort
is visibly
squared.
Above all when they look at each other.
When they stop and look at each other.

I confess
— she says with a sigh —
I haven't read Saussure.

Anyway the fascination
of Saussure
lies in the fact
that even someone who's read him
is not up to explaining him
(out loud) to others.

Morale:
una geniale
operazione
promozionale.
(Per capirlo devi leggerlo).

A Giorgio Celli.
Se l'amore
"è una forma sottile
di introspezione
per interposta persona"
— e lo è —
per proiezione
— se sei anche una superficie riflettente —
l'amore
ti renderà veggente.
P.S. Ormai, per interposta persona,
lo siamo in parecchi. Per fortuna.

Incontro per caso, inaspettatamente (dopo dieci anni che
non ci vediamo), Emilio Villa a Pavia.
A Pavia of all places
a cena alla *Cooperativa artigiani,*
gli chiedo se ricorda Nietzsche
in quella famosa foto con Lou Salomé (col frustino)
e con Paul Rée
e col carrettino.
Perché
— gli dico —
è un po' che cerco di collegare
i cavalli del *Paese degli Houyhnhnm* di Swift,
Lou Salomé col frustino,
Nietzsche (come cavallo?) davanti al carrettino
e Nietzsche che diventa "pazzo" a Torino
baciando un cavallo.
"Ah, ma allora", mi dice Emilio,
"devi risalire ai cavalli di Achille
che piangono lacrime
piagono calde lacrime
quando Patroclo muore..."
"Come se fossi in grado di farlo, Emilio..."
gli rispondo ridendo: "Vuoi scherzare?"

Moral:
a brilliant
promotional
gimmick.
(You have to read him to understand him.)

To Giorgio Celli.
If love
"is a subtle form
of introspection
by proxy"
— and it is —
by projection
— if you are also a reflective surface —
love
will render you clairvoyant
P.S. Now, by proxy,
we are in bunches. Fortunately.

By chance I meet, unexpectedly (after 10 years of not seeing
each other), Emilio Villa in Pavia.
In Pavia of all places
at dinner at the *Cooperativa artigiani,*
I ask if he remembers Nietzsche
in that famous photo with Lou Salome (with riding crop)
and with Paul Ree
and with the little cart.
Because
— I tell him —
it's a while I've been trying to connect
the horses of Swift's *Land of the Houyhnhnms,*
Lou Salome with riding crop,
Nietzsche (as horse?) in front of the little cart
and Nietzsche who goes "mad" in Turin
kissing a horse.
"Ah, but then", Emilio tells me
"you have to go back to the horses of Achilles
who wept tears
they wept hot tears
when Patroclus dies..."
"As if I was up to that, Emilio..."
I answer him laughing: "Are you kidding?"

Come può
questo scherzare
rimare
con *quel* collegare?
Reading it swiftly.

Se uno
avesse modo
di riascoltare
tutti i discorsi di Churchill
degli anni di guerra...
Chissà quanto Shakespeare
gli verrebbe incontro!

Mi hanno ormai nauseato
gli orologi nella pubblicità
che indicano sempre le 10 e 10.
Mai che indichino le 2 meno 10...
10 su 10, il massimo del voto.
10 e 10, le braccia alzate,
Gesù riceve la grazia.
Ne siamo così condizionati
che se la pubblicità ci mostrasse un orologio
che indica un'altra ora qualsiasi
probabilmente
ci sembrerebbe
privo di valore.
Comunque,
quando invece mi capita
di posare l'occhio
sul mio orologio da polso
proprio mentre sta segnando le 10 e 10...
mi vien da ridere,
o me lo porto all'orecchio
convinta che sia guasto.
Dai e dai,
ormai
questa fissazione delle 10 e 10 c'è.
Ed è irreversibile.
Pensa, T. S.
se il mondo
"not with a bang
but a whimper"
PROPRIO ALLE 10 e 10!

[100]

How can
this kidding
rhyme
with *that* connecting?
Reading it swiftly.

If one
had a way
to hear again
all of Churchill's speeches
during the war years...
Who knows how much Shakespeare
he'd come across!

By now they nauseate me
those watches in ads
that always show 10 after 10.
Never do they show 10 to 2...
10 out of 10, everytime.
10 out of 10, arms uplifted,
Jesus receives grace.
We are so conditioned
that if an ad showed us
a watch with whatever different time
probably
it would seem
not worth much.
Anyway,
when instead it happens
that my eye catches
my own watch
right while it's hitting 10 after 10...
I feel like laughing,
and I put it to my ear
convinced it's stopped.
Take it or leave it,
by now
you can't get away from 10 after 10.
And it's irreversible.
Think, T.S.
if the world
"not with a bang
but a whimper"
EXACTLY AT 10 AFTER 10!

Gli acciacchi della mezza età.
I primi dolorini qua e là
vengono
per distrarre dalla vita.
Così si è più pronti alla morte.

Anche la presbiopia
che viene verso i cinquanta
è un modo
di costringere la vista
a guardare lontano.

"Lasciatemi divertire"
diceva Palazzeschi
in momenti
come questi,
mesti.

Ogni tanto mi viene anche la voglia
di scrivere dei *Frisbees* cattivi.
Pieni di cattiveria.
Non lo faccio
solo per paura
che diventino dei boomerangs.

Scommetto che Rosellina Archinto
tiene la gigantografia di Goethe
dietro la scrivania del suo ufficio
anche per via di
"Röslein, Röslein, Röslein rot
Röslein auf der Heide..."

Nell'edizione Adelphi
le *101 storie Zen*
sono scritte su 110 pagine.
L'introduzione inizia a pagina 9.
Un tipografo Zen?

The infirmities of middle age.
The first little pains here and there
come
to distract from life.
So one will be more ready for death.

Even the far-sightedness
that comes around fifty
is a way
of forcing vision
to look far off.

"Let me have my fun"
said Palazzeschi
in moments
sad
as these.

Every once in a while I have the urge
to write some wicked *Frisbees*.
Full of wickedness.
I do not
only for fear
they'll turn into boomerangs.

I bet that Rosellina Archinto
keeps that giant picture of Goethe
behind the desk in her office
also because of
"Roeslein, Roeslein, Roeslein rot
Roeslein auf der Heide.". ."

In the Adelphi edition
the *101 Zen Stories*
are printed on 110 pages.
The introduction begins on page 9.
A Zen typographer?

Se, dopo aver letto i *Frisbees*,
la signora milanese
ha tentato nei miei confronti
quel suo maldestro colpo di vassallaggio
(ma, non potrei nemmeno giurare
che fosse consapevole di farlo),
questo vuol dire
che i *Frisbees* hanno suscitato in lei
il desiderio di mettermi in ginocchio.
Ma, non capisco,
l'ha fatto perché li ha capiti
o perché non li ha capiti?

Chiedo a Rosellina
se la mia intuizione
che riguarda lei e Goethe
è giusta. Ha un fondamento.
Giustamente
non mi risponde direttamente.
Mi dice che da bambina
lei diceva sempre:
"Röslein, Röslein, Röslein rot
Röslein über alles".

Il portavoce del presidente Reagan
si chiama Speakes?
How appropriate.

Cristiana Cohen
è un bel gioco di parole.

"Facciamo che:
Dante è vegetariano
e Shakespeare carnivoro".

"E Omero?"

"Ooom-ero
a modo uso
era cannibale".

If, after reading the *Frisbees,*
the Milanese signora
tried in my regard
that clumsy stroke of vassalage
(though I can't even swear
she was aware of it),
this must mean
the *Frisbees* aroused in her
the desire to put me on my knees.
But, I don't know,
did she do this because she understood them
or because she didn't?

I ask Rosellina
if my intuition
regarding her and Goethe
is right. Has a basis.
Justly
she doesn't answer me directly.
She tells me as a child
she always said:
"Roeslein, Roeslein, Roeslein rot
Roeslein über alles".

President Reagan's spokesman
is called Speakes.
How appropriate.

Christiana Cohen
is a nice play on words.

"Let's say that:
Dante is a vegetarian
and Shakespeare carnivorous".

"And Homer?"

"Hooom-er
was a cannibal
in his own little way."

A Luigi Pasotelli.

Per un certo periodo di tempo mi è stato detto che la più bella poesia che avevo scritto era *Como Trieste Venezia*. Questo titolo l'ha detto per primo Spatola.

Joan Arnold, Luigi Pasotelli e altri, mi hanno poi detto che la più bella poesia del poemetto *Singsong* è *Dencher Bag*. L'intera poesia è stata scritta da IS.

Giuliani, durante una lettura alla Galleria Giulia, vedendo in *Singsong* la pagina che riguarda Manganelli, mi disse che
L'intuizione migliore era quel: DESDEMONA   OTHELLO
l'intuizione migliore   DEMON   HELL
Questa intuizione la ebbe per prima Joan Arnold.

Morale: le mie poesie più belle sono di altri.

E le due suore
sedute di fronte a me
sul T.E.E.?

Mentre il treno si stacca da Stazione Termini
l'altoparlante nello scompartimento ci augura "Buon Viaggio!"
Le due suore alzano gli occhi al cielo?
                        all'altoparlante?
e all'unisono rispondono "Grazie!"

Questo è un *Frisbee,* di Dio,
di Fellini,
delle suore
o mio?

Per anni ho desiderato
mettere una raganella in un cucchiaio
e inghiottirla viva
come un tuorlo d'uovo.
(Quando lo confessavo agli amici
mi accorgevo che si scandalizzavano).
Solo da quando
— non più di un anno fa —
ho ricordato
che una raganella verdissima
dal ramo di un albero di frutta
mi pisciò in un occhio mentre la osservavo
(quando avevo quattro o cinque anni),
questo desiderio è passato.

Cari amici, a voi una rana ha mai pisciato in un occhio?

To Luigi Pasotelli.

For a certain time I was told that the best poem I'd written was *Como Trieste Venezia*. Spatola first said this title.

Joan Arnold, Luigi Pasotelli and others then told me that the most amusing section of the longer poem *Singsong* is *Dencher Bag*. The whole section was written by IS.

Giuliani, during a reading at the Galleria Giulia, seeing in *Singsong* the page referring to Manganelli, said that the best intuition was that: DESDEMONA   OTHELLO
              DEMON   HELL
Joan Arnold first had this intuition.

Moral: my best poems belong to others.

And the two nuns
seated facing me
on the T.E.E.?

While the train pulls out of the Termini Station
the loudspeaker in our compartment bids us "Bon Voyage!"
The two nuns raise their eyes to heaven? to the loudspeaker?
and in unison answer, "Thank you!"

Is this *Frisbee* God's,
Fellini's,
the nuns'
or mine?

For years I have wished
to put a frog on a spoon
and swallow it live
like an egg yolk.
(When I admitted this to friends
I realized they were shocked).
It was only after
— not more than a year ago —
I remembered
a very green frog
on a branch of a fruit tree
had pissed in my eye as I watched it
(when I was four or five years old),
that this desire passed.

Dear friends, has a frog ever pissed in your eye?

The salt of wisdom
is the spice of life.

New York, Halloween 1984
Dorothea Tanning
came to the door
looking like the devil
and said:
"The party is over".
She would not let us in.
My gratitude to her will be eternal.

Scrivo poesia
anche
per essere
più ascoltata.

Quest'ultima volta
gli Stati Uniti
mi sono apparsi
così trasparenti,
decifrabili...
E ho avuto
talmente tanta fede
negli Stati Uniti
che
tornata in Italia,
mi sono accorta
di averla persa tutta.

Ho cercato di scrivere le maiuscole
come me le hanno insegnate alle elementari.
(C'ero sempre riuscita).
Ma questa volta
me le sono sentite
remote ed estranee
come i dinosauri.
Si invecchia.

The salt of wisdom
is the spice of life.

New York, Halloween 1984
Dorothea Tanning
came to the door
looking like the devil
and said:
"The party is over"
She would not let us in.
My gratitude to her will be eternal.

I write poetry
also
to be listened to
a little more.

This last time
the United States
appeared to me
so transparent,
decipherable...
And I had
so much faith
in the United States
that
back in Italy,
I became aware
of having lost it all.

I tried to write capitals
as I was taught in school.
(I always managed).
But this time
they felt
remote and estranged
like dinosaurs.
One grows old.

All'inizio
mi sono augurata
che i *Frisbees*
mi aiutassero
a far funzionare il cervello
in modo nuovo.
Cosa è cambiato?

Adesso ho più paura di prima.
Peccato. Peccato.

Aprile 1982 – Aprile 1985

At the start
I hoped
the *Frisbees*
would help
my mind to work
in a new way.
What has changed?

Now I am more afraid than before.
What a shame.

April 1982 — April 1985

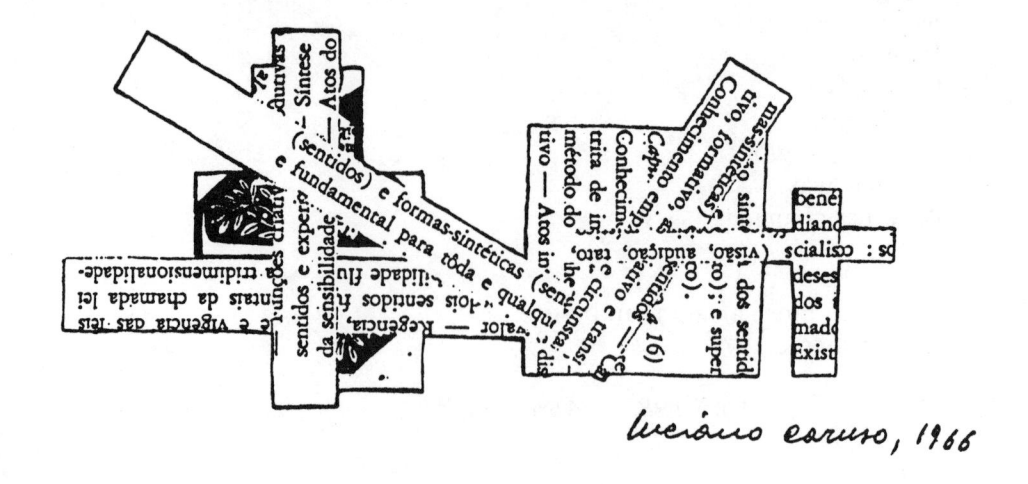

luciano caruso, 1966

LUCIANO CARUSO

LUCIANO CARUSO was born in Naples in 1944, where he lived until moving to Florence in 1976. He has published several volumes of linear poems, including *Chronica de Parthenope (poesie 1965/ 1967)* in 1977, excerpted here, as well as numerous volumes of visual/concrete poetry, object & artist's books. Since the 60s, Caruso has been an editor of avant-garde publications, among them *Linea Sud, Ana etcetera, Continuum, Uomini e idea* and *Visual Art Center.* He has also published extensively as a scholar and critic of visual poetry, from the Middle Ages to the historical and contemporary avant-gardes. Currently he directs the series of art publications, *Le brache di Gutenberg,* Belforte Editore (Livorno).

This selection has been translated by Paul Vangelisti, with the help of Ippolita Rostagno.

CHRONICA DE PARTHENOPE

a miradois salgono i gradoni
— il nuovo corso della poesia
prego comm. nacchennella
perché il verso sciolto ILLUSIONE
     l'uomo fratello a castelnuovo
      ciccio coppola d'amalfi —
la città sul vuoto dall'ultimo colera — gran mistero
scavato senza amore
     sorride nello sguardo attrappito
napoli sacra presso un libraro — prenotarsi —
unico e solo nella capitale
     (schiera di santi in copertina
      con tunica e pallio
biancovestiti
nella sinistra il libro delle entrate e uscite —
salvatore cepparulo fecit)
in alto l'origine secentesca del reale
      con tracce superstiti d'affresco
      terminale d'ambulacro
esplicito senso ornamentale — cemeterium
     (alle fontanelle madonna della vita)
— nell'archivio l'epitaffio grida la musa personale
      dal tempo di sicone langobardo
urbs parthenope et henneapolitanis
      falsidici viri
(fronte a strada palazzo pappacoda in controluce)

multilaterale nel tufo a gallerie
     le cantarelle almeno questo
in una guida alla città
    il discorso ti accarezza in tutta reverenza
col ricordo dei primi mercatanti nel regno
— da solo quella strana figura del gran siniscalco
seduto contemplava il bel mondo in san lorenzo —
(petrarca il solito ciclone alla sua porta)
      a pianta ellittica la chiesa
manomorta id est privilegium
a favore di un priore fiorentino
     — notevole esempio di moderno mercatante
     l'acciaiuoli il giglio nella mano

CHRONICA DE PARTHENOPE

at miradois the big steps climb
— the new path of poetry
pray capt. readyrump
because blank verse ILLUSION
                the man brother at castelnuovo
                ciccio coppola of amalfi —
the city void from the last cholera — great mystery
excavated without love
                smiles in the numb glance
sacred naples in care of a bookseller — make reservations —
unique and alone in the capitol
                (swarm of saints on the cover
                with tunic and pallium
dressedinwhite
in his left hand the ledger —
salvatore cepparulo fecit)
high up the 17th century origin of the real
                with surviving traces of fresco
                end of an ambulatory
explicit ornamental taste — cimeterium
                (at the fontanelle madonna della vita)
— in the archive the epitaph cries out the personal muse
                from the time of sicone longobard
urbs parthenope et henneapolitanis
                falsidici viri
(front of the street palazzo pappacorda against the light)

multilateral in the tunnelled pumice
                the burial nooks* this at least
in a city guidebook
            the talk caresses you in all reverence
with memory of the first merchants in the kingdom
— that strange figure alone the great finance minister
seated contemplating the good life in san lorenzo —
(petrarch the usual cyclone at his door)
                the church with elliptical ground plan
manomorta id est privilegium
in favor of a florentine priest
            — noteworthy example of the modern merchant
            acciaiuoli the fleurs de lys in his hand

*Niches in Neopolitan catacombs in which the dead are
buried vertically, in the walls, with heads exposed.

intanto a castelnuovo ciccio coppola coi figli
dietro i miracoli a sinistra
            a miradois si sale per gradoni
e il discorso all'antiuomo — in questo luogo
                    federico per lo studio — gloria del regno
                    che non ardiscano (il duca d'alba si scaldava
                    nelle piazze di toledo)
                    locare nelle loro case
                        IL BANDO
                    donne corteggiane studenti et altre persone
                    dissoneste
                    per quanto hanno cara la gratia de la Maestà
                    sotto pena di docati dui milia
                    et altre pene anco corporali
                    ad arbitrio di sua eccellenza — datum neapoli
pezzo di vita elaborato apriva le braccia
                  nelle carte dell'archivio invero
alla luce dell'arte divus Januarius
(il santo patrono rapito da sicone beneventano)
                  lungo poema
il ritmo interno della silloge documentaria
— scendeva per via chiaia il nume tutelare
                  alcoolizzato
(sul tavolo chiaro all'accademia
dopo ogni crociata — pazzariello locale & C.
nel regno signore di nove città)

di notte per tutta la collina
intenti alla finestra — ma non era divertente —
            il tono al grande archivio con il resto
sui quartieri tavole azzurre nel naufragio
            l'anonimo cantore
inchiodato al dipinto nella casa dei viceré
— incompleto (la fine dei marranos nel regno) —
conosco l'augurio :
            l'incantevole rischio della maldicenza
sul fare del mattino
                con la chitarra del picaro vicino —
                    l'amico americano a cinépresa
                    sguscia negli angoli seduto

in the meantime at castelnuovo ciccio coppola with his children
behind miracoli on the left
          at miradois you by the big steps
and talk against the antiman — in this place
              federico in favor of study — glory of the kingdom
              that they not dare (the duke of alba warmed himself
              in the piazzas of toledo)
              let their houses
                  THE DECREE.
              courtesans students and other persons
              dishonest
              because they hold dearly the graces of his majesty
              under penalty of ducats two-thousand
              and even other corporal punishments
              at his excellency's caprice — datum neapoli
elaborate piece of life he opened his arms
              in truth in pages of archive
in light of the art divus Januarius
(the patron saint kidnapped by sicone from benevento)
                      long poem
the internal rhythm of the documentary volumes
— the guardian angel was descending by way of via chiaia
                          drunk
(on the clear slab at the academy
after every crusade — the fool & co.
in the kingdom of nine cities

at night all across the hill
intent at the window — but it wasn't fun —
              the tone at the great archive with the rest
on the quarters the azure tablets in the shipwreck
              the anonymous cantor
nailed to the painting in the viceroys' house
incomplete (the end of marranos in the kingdom)
— I know those best wishes :
              the enticing risk of slander
at daybreak
      with a copy of the picaresque guitar nearby —
                      the american friend slips
                      from corner to corner sitting
                      as if in a film

                              — bianco il pensiero del suo amore
                              ferito a morte senza uguale
                              in mezzo spaccanapoli l'amico
                              fermo nell'ombra razionale che fa addio
(attività mitopoietica : la salvezza con gli altri)
                    le cose che diceva ai capitelli in santaspreno —

ma la memoria è una strana interferenza :
il bel cortile cinquecentesco
                — portale del sanfelice barocco —
palazzo filomarino illuminato
                in un giorno dell'anno 1722
giambattista vico teneva conferenza
a principi e baroni (il passato
e domini gratia la istoria tutta quello che insomma
                            a noi era rimasto
— in giro il volgo di qualsiasi sorta
                correva ai primi posti —
convenendo che la verità discoverta
con molto travaglio e diligentia
per lecito e onesto sollazzo
sia consultata all'infermi di mente)
nella stagione morta napoli nobilissima
— scritto a boustrophedon — l'inserto della crisi

                    — white the thought of his love
                    wounded to death without comparison
                    in the middle of spaccanapoli still
                        the friend in the rational shade who waves goodbye
(mythopoetic activity : salvation along with the others)
                    the things he said to the capitals in santaspreno —

but memory is a strange interference :
the nice 16th century courtyard
                            — door of the baroque sanfelice —
palazzo filomarino illuminated
                on a day in the year 1722
gianbattista vico lectured
to princes and barons (the past
and domini gratia and all of history which in fact
                                    was left us
— around the populace of all sorts
                    ran to the first seats —
agreed that the truth discovered
with much travail and diligence
for lawful and honest sport
be conferred upon the infirm of mind)
in the dead season most noble naples
— written in boustrophedon — the insertion of crisis

MENTRE LA NOTTE DAL DOLCE VOLTO DI LUNA

oh benny lasciala ti prego — faccio le valigie
                         ti dico torno a casa
i bambini di nuovo oh benny — non eri appeso
e senza mosche — sulla litorale
ferma benny c'è una casa — sorride
i pomeriggi specialmente — a largo dei francesi
                             una domenica sotto l'arco
— io osservo benny le gambe di tua moglie
a rete nera troppo scoperta e dorme
per l'ultima volta colpisci benny
                         più forte — ti osservo benny
la morte sulle scale capisci dagli occhi
mi perdi benny non sei capace benny a grottaromana
le sere d'estate — volevi scrivere nonsobene
                            una commedia con la tuta azzura —
di giorno e stanotte oh benny benny è tardi
— le mani in tasca — hai le calze bagnate cretina
                         corriamo dammi il braccio
tuo marito a quest'ora per casa — che c'entra
                           oh benny non riesce a parlare
scusa se rido croce bianca croce nera
qui sulle foglie ma è freddo — appunto
che c'importa se il camion era morto
mica vero benny coniglio ti compro il trombone
(giri a destra poi a sinistra c'è una piazza la strada di fronte)
                           ti perdevi benny anche nella tua città
— ho trovato il coraggio benny è inutile che fai quella faccia
ti telefono dall'ufficio sai —
— la casa nuova al terzo piano — col tetto di legno
gli occhi di tua moglie — non ti guarda benny
                        rossa in faccia per la febbre
oddio benny sulla litorale che non riesci più a cantare
meglio lasciarsi prima che — prima cosa
                     dicevi di amarmi — certo che
                     è solo un'esperienza — vuoi capire
                     io mi ammazzo benny — e c'eri anche
tu benny — io ti osservo benny seduto da una parte
il sole in un angolo del tavolo —
                       fai finta di niente

WHILE THE NIGHT ON THE SWEET FACE OF THE MOON

oh benny leave her I beg you — I'll pack my bags
                        I tell you I'm going back home
the children again oh benny — you weren't left hanging
or without flies — along the boardwalk
stop benny there's a house — she smiles
the afternoons especially — on largo dei francesi
                          a Sunday under the arch
— I observe benny your wife's legs
in black net too exposed and she sleeps
for the last time you lash out benny
                                harder — I observe you benny
death on the steps you understand from the eyes
you're losing me benny you're incapable benny in grottaromana
summer evenings — you wanted to write I don't know
                          a comedy in blue overalls —
by day and tonight oh benny benny it's late
— hands in the pockets — your stockings are wet stupid
                        let's run give me your arm
your husband by now at home — so what
                          oh benny unable to speak
sorry if I'm laughing white cross black cross
here on the leaves but it's cold — exactly
what do we care if the truck died
not true benny rabbit I'll buy you a trombone
(turn right then left there's a square the street straight ahead)
                    you'd get lost benny even in your own city
— I've found courage benny it's no use making that face
I'm calling from the office you know —
— the new house on the third floor — with a wooden roof
your wife's eyes — she doesn't look at you benny
                            face red with fever
oh god benny on the boardwalk that you're not able to sing anymore
better to leave each other before — before you used to
                    say you loved me — of course
                    it's just an experience — you understand
                    I'm going to kill myself benny — and you there
too benny — I observe you benny sitting off to the side
the sun on a corner of the table —
                        you pretend it's nothing

miranapoli di fianco e la musica oh benny perché
— handicap nel respiro del mio — cosa?
                    solo l'inferno e la morte (discendente)
                    meglio così non dar retta
— muorto è lo purpo e sta sott'a la preta
muorto è ser janni figlio di poeta —

LE STANZE DELL'AMORE SERIALE

che: dal libro del Celano (del bello dell'antico
e del curioso contenuto) — adesso
per le piazze un viso ripetuto e/
                    il letto capisco
col mio amore : et dulcis (maniera) che non trovo altro modo
il pianto (nel liber) e la nostra vita
                    (ancora) che il desiderio del canto spiegato
in una casa — narcissus (dal nomen) senza più grido:
o cura d'arricchire // ai prezzi del mercato corrente (sentimento)
nella città — la pietra del sogno perfetto
            se il mito capituli e privilegi
            — l'unico aspetto concesso //
: humile facies — per la serie e lo stampo diverso un mattino
ne' l'archivio de la Sacra Neapolitana Ecclesia — che poi:
                    // dalla stanza dell'amore seriale
                    affidata a un cartografo a stampa
                    e l'urlo di chiaro colore (poi) :
che sono partito da mia casa con altre persone
                    (se una storia bellissima)
                    : diversamente da quanto —
et andai a roma all'età di anni undeci in circa
                    archi rampanti e il delirio preciso
                    dal quadro — che solo a bottega
dove m'imparai l'arte predetta (per la illustrissima città)
nel paese barocco — e quando in tal modo sarà scesa la domanda
muteranno anche i prezzi /
                    / in attesa di linee complete —
nella stanza (i suoi occhi e un gesto in primo piano)

miranapoli over there and the music oh benny why
— handicap in the breathing of my — what?
                     only hell and death (descending)
                     better like this let it sit
— dead is the octopus in the stone crypt
dead is master janni son of the poet —

THE ROOMS OF SERIAL LOVE

from the book of Celano (of the pretty and antique
and of curious content) — now
in the piazzas a repeated face/
                     the bed I understand
with my love : et dulcis (manner) I find no other way
the weeping (nel liber) and our life
                     (again) a voce piena
in a house — Narcissus (from nomen) with no cry left:
or concern for getting rich // at current market prices (sentiment)
in the city — the stone of the perfect dream
         if the myth law and privilege
           — the only aspect conceded —
: humile facies — for the different series and molds one morning
in the archive of the Sacra Neapolitana Church — that then:
                   // from the room of serial love
                   given in custody to a map printer
                   and the scream of light color (then):
that I left my house with other people
            (if a wonderful story)
            : different from what —
and I went to Rome at the age of about eleven
               rampant arch and the delirium precise
               from the painting — that only in the shop
where I learned the predicted art (for that very illustrious city)
in the baroque country — and when demand in that way will have declined
even the prices will change /
             / waiting for complete lines —
in the room (her eyes and a movement in the foreground)

ancora possibile // e solo nei casi di monopolio
: firmato / françois de nomé di lorena e proprio di mez
et tre anni sono che mi ritrovo habitare qui
et non ho padre
— che l'odore di morte dall'enunciato poema (comentario)
intorno al reggimento delle piazze e rue nella città
(dopo sua morte) da tutti dimandato monsù desiderio
per strano motivo // dove ciascuno di essi determina
: ma /
      l'oggetto nel giorno della mia morte
per le strade del centro
                       // calcolando: in numero pari alle possibiltà
sul grande cortile tuttora esistente — dal tempo che partii da mia casa
                             mai ho avuto avviso se è viva o è morta
per la linea dei ricordi e inutile (amore) tutta la notte
e maggiore richiamo : esemplare / dalla vita che un ritorno
o un lungo rimpianto
              (agli atti d'ufficio in questa città)
i resti della vuota leggenda — ancora // atteso che io la lassai viva
                         quando partii da mia casa —

still possible // and only in cases of monopoly
: signed / françois de nomé of lorena and actually of mez
and it is three years I find myself living here
and have no father
— that the smell of death from the enunciated poem (commentary)
around the regiment in the piazzas and rues of the city
(after his death) by all called monsù desiderio*
for strange reason // where each of them determines
: but /
      the object on the day of my death
in the streets in the center
                        // calculating: in number equal to the possibilities
in the grand courtyard still extant — from the time I left home never
                        have I been told if she was alive or dead
for the line of memories is futile (love) all night long
and a greater call: example / from life that a return
or a long regret
        (in the official records of this city)
the remains of empty legend — again // I swear I left her alive
                        when I went from my house —

*The speaker is the infamous Neopolitan painter, Monsù Desiderio, who, it was later discovered, was the fabrication of two other painters, Didier Barra and Francois de Nomé.

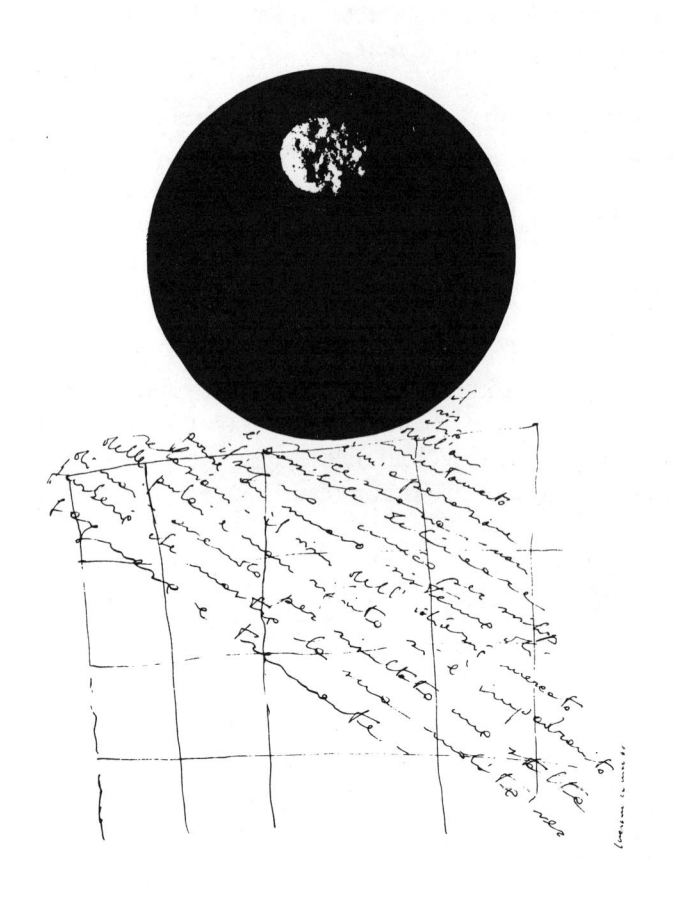

POESIA (1967)

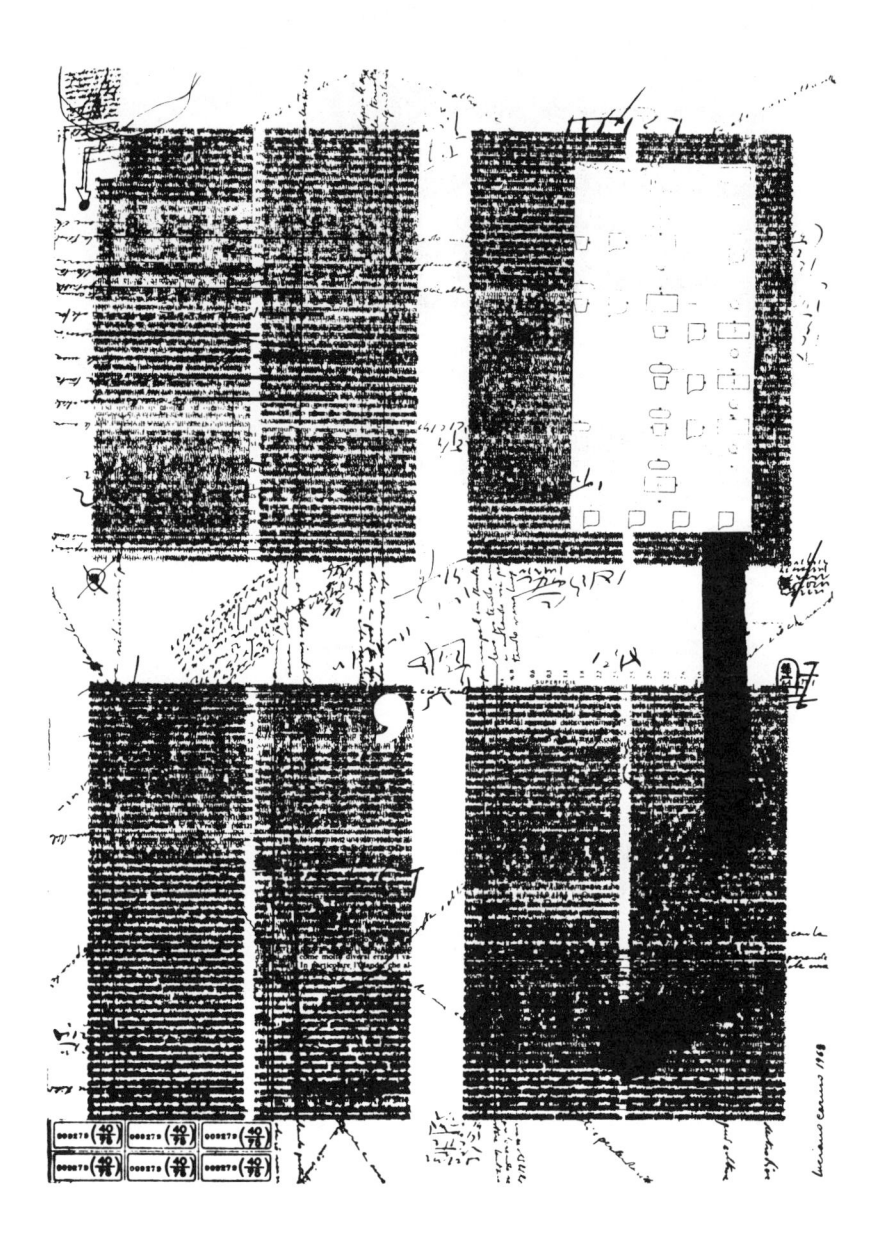

TABULA (1968)

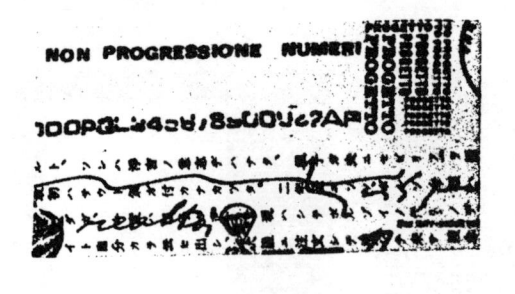

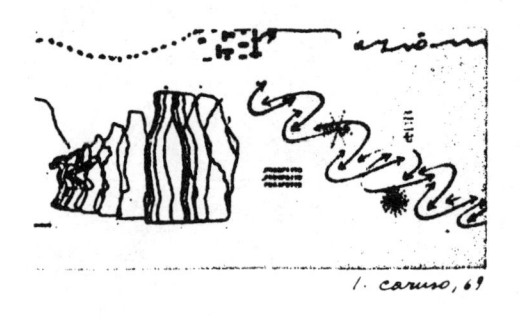

PROGETTO (1969)

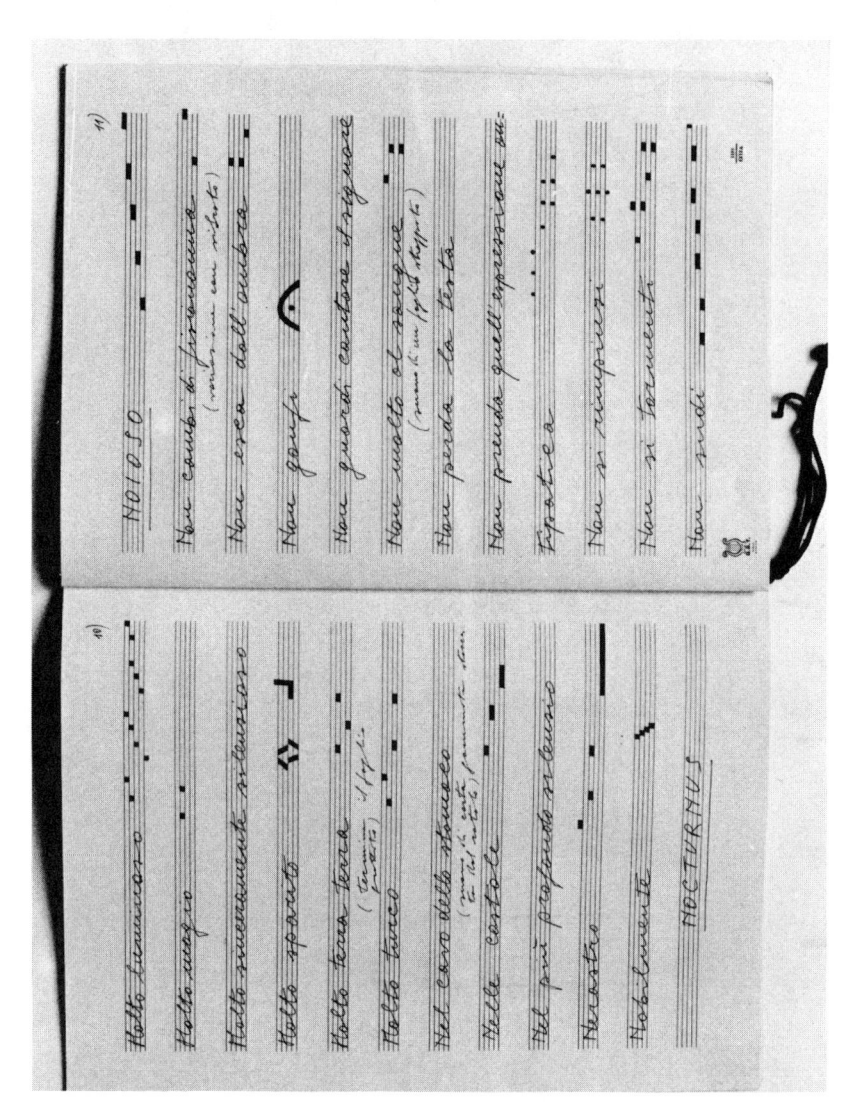

LIBRO DI MUSICA / LITOGRAMMI (1971-1975)
(turn clockwise)

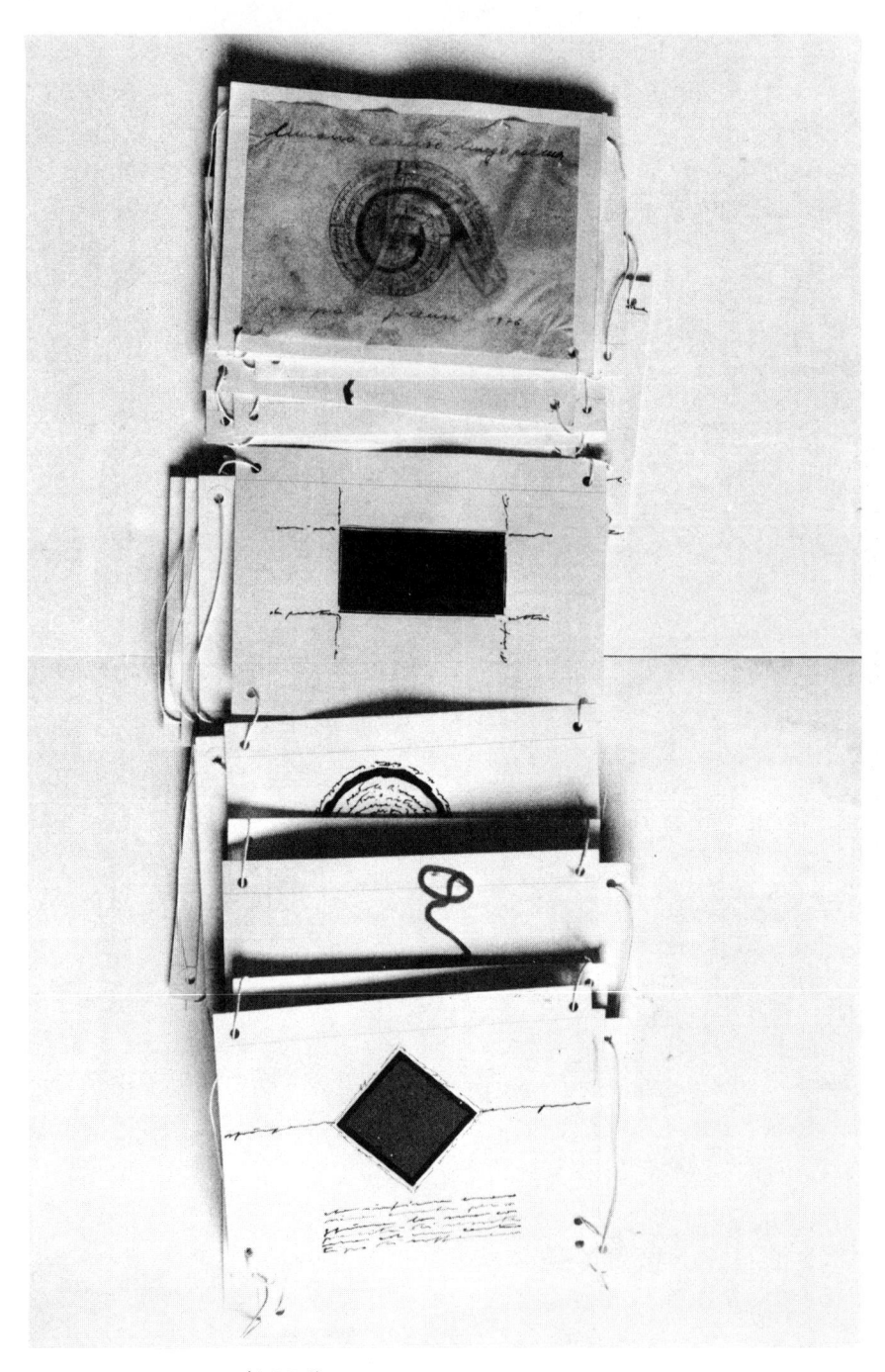

LUNGO POEMA (1976)

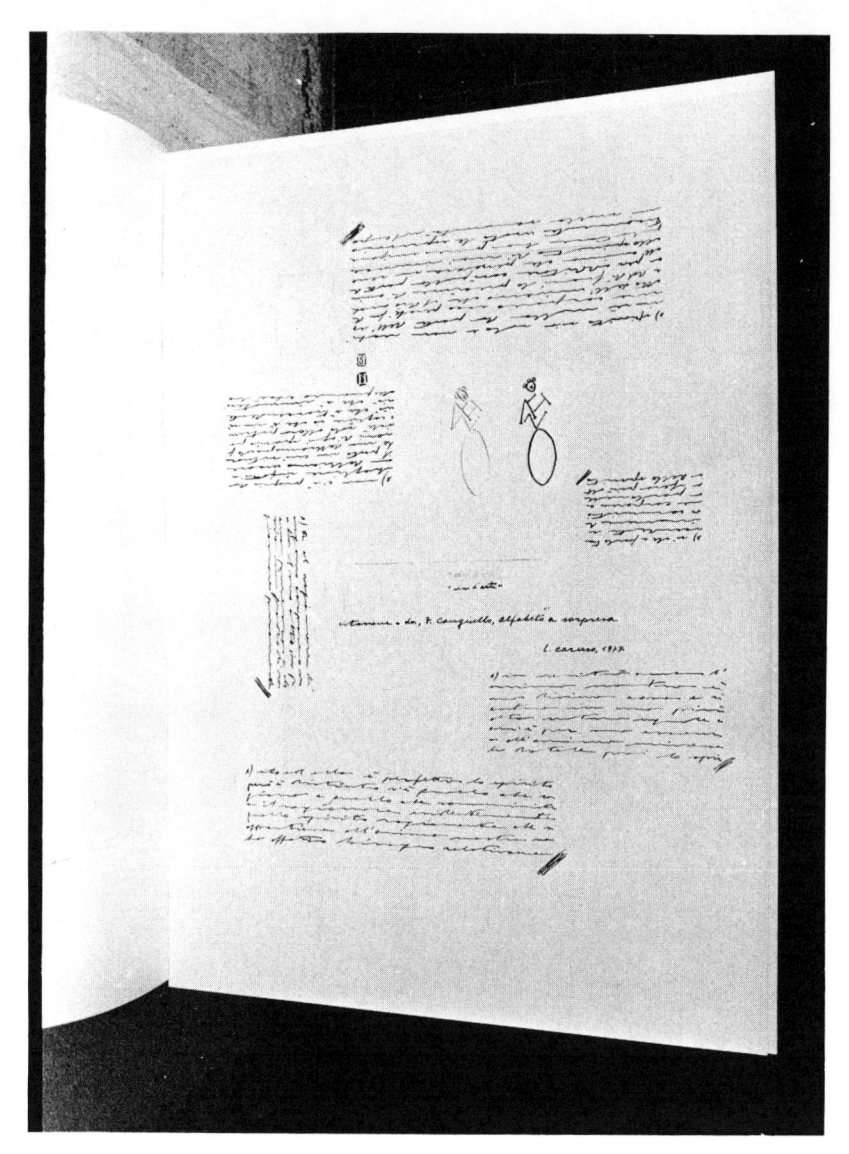

CITAZIONE (1977)

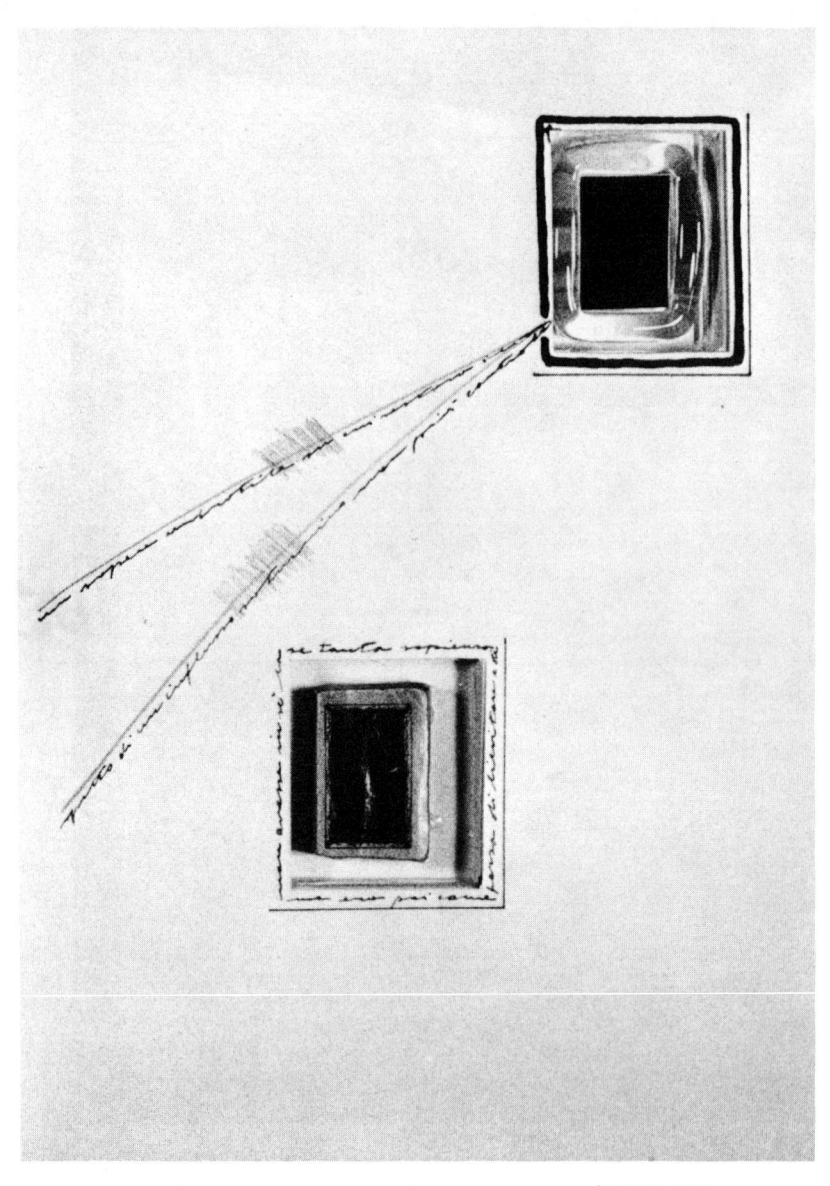

HISTOIRE D'AMOUR POUR S'EN MOURIR (1977-78)

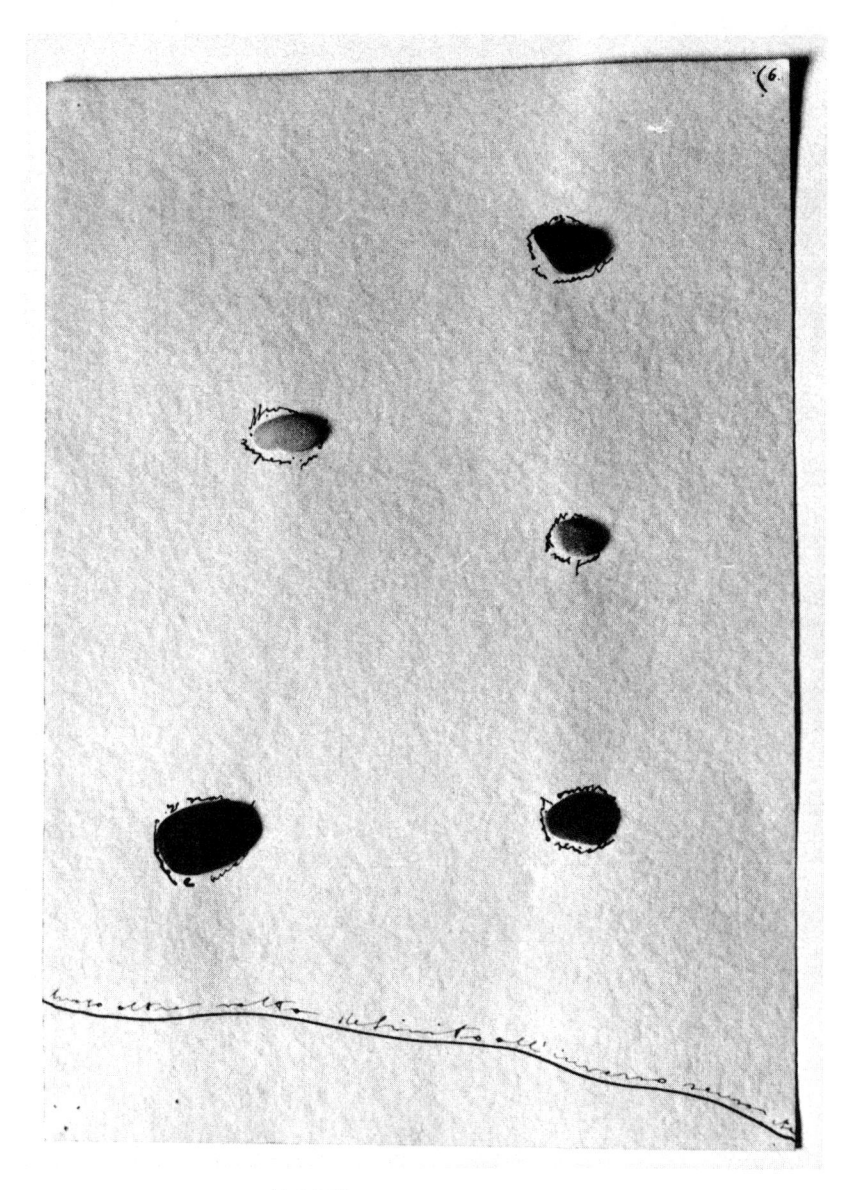

LIBRO SEGRETO (1983)

DE/SCRITTURA (lettera per...)

e qui niente – l'ossessione – il nulla – niente dei nostri sogni
      /le carte morte dell'archivio e i segni/
: ho ripresso a camminare sai a respirare anche
      : e incontrandoti piú pallido e perso nei tuoi occhi
            : usurpando la tristezza vera di un altro
                        : che io ero/ risentito

: e dirò son questo e son quello
                  /qualòra: con tono minaccioso/
il dolore dell'alba fra note sparse e frammenti e buio di pensieri
                  /le carte fiorite al margine/
girando tra ombre e ombre – languor naturae – e lo scrivere alto
appassionato : e seguire il filo di una voce
                  : nel labirinto di ogni giorno
                  : moins que nul : leurs ombres ont
leurs couleurs / e alzarsi e andare incontro a qualcuno sulla porta /
: l'offerta del pane –
            ma è questa la saggezza? questo vuol dire
/ aprendo gli occhi/
            siamo cresciuti e diventati grandi? e certo
ogni cosa che esiste è luce :
                  ma solo come se – per gioco –
                        o nelle parole dell'amore ...

[134]

DE/SCRIPTURE (letter for...)

and here nothing — obsession — emptiness — nothing of our dreams
                                      /the dead pages of the archive and the signs
: I've started walking again you know and breathing even
                       : and meeting you more pallid and lost in your eyes
                                  : usurping the true sadness of another
                                                    : who I was/ resentful
: and I'd say that I am this and that
                           /occasionally: with menacing tone/
the pain of the dawn among scattered notes and fragments and darkness of thought
                                                        /the pages blooming at the edges/
turning between shadows and shadows — languor naturae — and the writing lofty
passionate: and to follow the thread of a voice
                                 : in the labyrinth of each day
                                 : moins que nul: leurs ombres ont
leurs couleurs/ and to rise and meet someone at the door/
: the offer of bread —
                      but is this wisdom? this means
/ opening your eyes/
              have we grown up and come of age? and certainly
all that is is light:
                    but only as if — in a joke —
                    or in words of love...

IN ATTESA DELLA NOTTE

"NOX *dicitur ab eo quod humanis noceat negotiis*"
(Vergilio Grammatico — Epitomi XI, 5)

è il silenzio dell'alba che spaventa /
                          rovine &
fughe di sale e di palazzi a spaccanapoli
                        — oh i grandi portali
spesi all'apparenza — nel giorno che viene
non si sentono uccelli dai giardini o foglie o voci
— per strada il vuoto di memorie — il mio amico
lui il commediante che sognava nobiltà di tratto
nei titoli di un film o un uomo altero dal dipinto
: certo fuori del suo tempo — jadis
dans l'un des paniers c'est moi que l'on mettait —
il bello è difficile — non si conosce né importa
come sia finita la supplica di giovan battista vico
al giovane re — cantos CXVI — il palinsesto
: anch'io amai la quiete e la luminescenza remota
lasciando che un altro vivesse al mio posto /
et ego boni vice hospitii — prostrato —
prostrato ai vostri reali piedi eccetera
supplicando eccetera la maestà vostra
                          umilissimamente /
le rappresenta ch'esso è il più anziano
di questi pubblici studi avendo tutti gli altri
lettori cominciato ad avervi catedre per assienti
de' tempi appresso — dalla sua casa d'angolo infino
al portale della gloriosa biblioteca affidata
ai gerolomini pensava al modo — una protesta —
o forse parlava da solo a voce alta — e perché
essendo per ordine reale esposta tutta l'università
ad un generale concorso tre sole catedre
                        non furono opposte /
in tutto questo gran spazio di tempo esso supplicante
non ha quasi mai lasciato passar annon nel quale
non avesse dato alla luce alcun opera
                        del suo povero ingegno
— il bello certo è difficile — si tu n'y as jamais —
e tenerlo legato con le parole dell'amore —
dal trattato tenuto in gran conto nella biblioteca
: un lungo affanno —

WAITING FOR THE NIGHT

> *"so it may be said* NIGHT *is harmful to human affairs"*
> (Vergilius Grammaticus, Epitomes, XI, 5)

it is the silence of dawn that frightens /
                                  ruins &
fugue of rooms and buildings at spaccanapoli
                                  — oh the big portals
worn in appearance — in the coming day
we don't hear birds from the gardens or leaves or voices
— in the street the emptiness of memory — my friend
he the comedian who dreamt of noble gestures
in the titles of a film or a haughty man in the painting
: certainly out of his time — jadis
dans l'un des paniers c'est moi que l'on mettait —
beauty is difficult — we don't know nor does it matter
how giovan battista vico's supplication to the young king
turned out — canto CXVI — the palimpsest
: I too loved the quiet and the remote luminescence
given that another live in my place /
et ego boni vice hospitii — prostrated —
prostrated at your royal feet, etcetera
begging etcetera your majesty
                     most humbly /
representing that he is the eldest
in these public studies all the other readers
having commenced to have chairs for assienti
in subsequent years — from his house on the corner to
the glorious library in custody
of the order of st jerome he thought of the way — a protest —
or maybe he was talking to himself outloud — and because
by royal order the whole university being exposed
to a general examination only three chairs
                              were not contested /
in all this great span of time he supplicant
has never let pass a year in which
he did not give birth to a work
                      of his poor genius
— beauty is certainly difficult — si tu n'y as jamais —
and to keep it fast with the words of love —
from the tract held in great esteem in the library
: a long sufferance

il vostro progresso durato lo spazio di un mattino /
delle quali v'ha un catalogo nel tomo primo della
raccolta degli opuscoli eruditi /
                              ora il supplicante
si truova in grave età con numerosa famiglia
e poverissimo avendo dalla sua atcedra più di soldo
che cento scudi annui con altri pochi incerti
ch'essigge dal diritto delle fedi di rettorica
che dà ai giovani /
e meditò in seguito i princìpi di una scienza nuova
d'intorno alla comune natura delle nazioni
— mais je ne savais pas qu'avait surgi la lune —
della quale l'abate ...nti senza esseri conosciuti
gli scrive che nell'italiana favella non sia uscito
libro che contenga più cose erudite e filosofiche
e queste tutte originali nella specie loro
e di averne mandato un picciolo estratto in francia
: il cielo ha già il colore intenso dell'autunno —
le nuvole di nuovo i loro contorni definiti si muovono
cambiano le forme ed un vento leggero agita le foglie
maintenant que presque plus personne au monde
                                          ne m'aime
: il tuo profumo di violetta ma leggermente più
penetrante e pungente si mescola all'etereo e dolce
miele della labularia maritima — maintenant /
                              c'était moi qui aurais
voulu pleurer — per tutto ciò priega la maestà vostra
a degnarsi d'impiegarlo nella carica di vostro istorico
regio con tanto di sostentamento che unito con quello
della catedra possa con qualche riposo
scrivere le vostre gloriosissime geste
e finire onestamente la vita — in napoli giugno
1734 — e stanchi occhi al mattino —
quello che si vede dalla sala di lettura — dopo
i tre gradini — tremulis ab umbris —
il sole qui nasce di fianco dalla collina
: il tempo non è — il tempo è male — dicevo nel cortile
in controluce — poco più di un profilo /
                              la linea di un cammeo
nel castello di vatolla — dal suo studio il mare lontano
che fa orizzonte — una linea più chiara nella stanza
e vele nere — richiamo o sogno che passa — oh le nuvole

your progress lasted the space of one morning /
of which we have a catalog in the first tome of the
collection of erudite monographs /
                              now the supplicant
discovers himself at a grave age with numerous family
and very poor having from his chair but
an hundred escudos annual and few uncertain others
which he exacts from the right of rhetorical examination
that he gives to the young /
and he meditated subsequently upon the principles of a new science
concerning the common nature of nations
— mais ne savait pas qu'avait sourgi la lune —
of which the abbot ...nti never having met him
writes that in the italian tongue there never appeared
book that contained more erudite and philosophical things
and these all original in their kind
and that he had sent a small extract to france
: already the sky holds the intense color of fall —
the clouds anew move their definite contours
changing shapes and a slight breeze agitates the leaves
maintenant que presque plus personne au monde
                                         ne m'aime
: your perfume of violets but slightly more
penetrating and pungent mixes with the ethereal and sweet
honey of the labularia maritima — maintenant /
                               c'etait moi qui aurais
voulu pleurer — for all this I pray your majesty
to deign to employ him in the service of your historical
rule with as much as a salary which together with that
of the chair he may with some repose
write of your glorious acts
and end his life honestly — in naples june
1734 — and tired eyes in the morning —
that which we see from the reading room — beyond
the three steps — tremulis ab ombris —
here the sun is born along the hillside
: the weather is not — the weather is evil — I said in the courtyard
against the light — little more than a profile /
                              the line of a cameo
in the castle of vatolla — from his studio the far sea
forms the horizon — a brighter line in the room
and black sails — call or dream that passes — oh the clouds

a primavera o in un settembre luminoso — risolvilo /
risolvilo tu stesso il problema del tuo cuore —
                    in un momento d'abbandono /
qualche volta voleva parlare — e certo li strapazzi
dell'avversa fortuna "per rendere i letterati neghittosi
di ricercare un libro vano falso d'un autor sconosciuto" —
ancora nel dicembre del 1740 — ai padri conservatori
della biblioteca dei gerolomini bisognerà consigliare
di cercare scritti proibiti nelle legature dei libri
ammessi o più recenti — venez ici je vous ai ouvert
les portes — il ritmo interno del respiro — di nuovo
giovan battista vico istoriografo regio e professore
d'eloquenza ne' regi studi prostrato ai piedi eccetera
umilmente eccetera / supplicandola esprime a la sacra
real maestà come esso da quaranta e più anni ha servito
e serve in questa regia università col tenue soldo
                              — ut supra —
di cento ducati annui co' quali miseramente ha dovuto
sostentar sé e la sua povera famiglia e perché ora
è giunto in un'età assai avanzata / era l'ora quieta
— un presagio anche — sospeso — estne sacerdos intus —
aeternis in lusibus omnis —
             / ed è aggravato e quasi oppresso
da tutti que' mali che gli anni e le continue fatighe
sofferte soglion seco portare e soprattutto è stretto
dall'angustie domestiche e dalli strapazzi dell'avversa
fortuna da' quali sempre ed ora più che mai
troppo crudelmente viene malmenato — vivendo diceva
in uno stato di sospensione — sacris errabat in umbris
: e le notizie che arrivavano dai gerolomini non erano
buone ché la sala grande era guasta dall'umido e
dalla pioggia che entrava dal tetto — nulla ha valore
solo la qualità e nessuno dentro che porti rancore —
— e qualche stipo in alto minacciava di crollare —
una separatezza rassegnata che proprio per questo era
sempre più rappresentativa di una condizione — at quasi
per nebulam — che stava diventando la condizione umana —
un rovescio di pioggia — ci fermammo sorpresi di fronte
alla sua lapide /
             la differenza ricordava — idest nomen —
per l'acquisto consigliato — si aggiunse al fondo inizale
la famosa raccolta — per intervento diretto — i quali mali

in the spring or in a luminous september — resolve it /
you yourself resolve the problem of your heart —
                    in a moment of abandon /
and sometimes he wanted to talk — and surely the hardships
of hard luck "to render the literary slothful
in searching out a vain and false book by author unknown" —
still in december of 1740 — the father conservators
of the jeromian library must be advised to be
on the lookout for prohibited writings in bindings of approved
or more recent books — venez ici je vous ai ouvert
les portes — the internal rhythm of breath — again
giovan battista vico historiographer and professor
of oratory in royal studies prostrated at the feet etcetera
humbly etcetera / supplicating he explains to his sacred
royal majesty how for forty and more years he has served
and is serving in this royal university with the scanty pay
                                        — ut supra —
of a hundred ducats annual with which he has had to wretchedly
support himself and his poor family and since now
he has reached a sufficiently advanced age / it was the quiet hour
— an omen even — hanging — estne sacerdos intus —
aeternis in lusibus omnis —
            / and is weighed down and almost oppressed
by all those ailments that the years and the constant toil
suffered are wont to bring with them and above all afflicted
by domestic hardships and the fatigue of ill
fortune always by which and now more than ever
he is too harshly battered — living he said
in a state of suspension — sacris errabat in umbris
: and the news that came from the jeromians was not
good because the large hall was wasted by the humidity
and rain seeping in from the roof — nothing has value
only quality and nobody inside who may bear a grudge —
— and some cabinet on high threatening to fall —
a resigned apartness that precisely for this was
all the more characteristic of a condition — at quasi
per nebulam — that was becoming the human condition —
a cloudburst — we stopped surprised in front
of his grave /
            the difference reminded of — idest nomen —
for the proposed acquisition — the famous collection was added
to the original sum — by direct intervention — which ills

del corpo — che certe immagini poi si formino nella mente
per rimanervi — accompagnati ed uniti ai più potenti
quali sono quelli dell'animo l'hanno reso
in uno stato affato inabile per la vita —
                              non potendo più
trascinare il corpo già stanco e quasi cadente
per la qual cosa si è veduto nella necessità di sostituire
in suo luogo interinamente nella catedra della rettorica
un suo figliuolo il quale — nigra absconditur umbra —
da più anni s'ha indossato il peso di questa carica
con qualche soddisfazione del pubblico — une nuit entière
— il devait rester dans l'ombre — pour que je puisse
lire ma chance parmi les étoiles /
                  — per rimanere o per definire —
del che ne può essere bastante pruova il mantenersi
l'istessa udienza o l'istesso concorso dei giovani
che esso supplicante soleva avere e perché esso già
si vede in età cadente e dall'angustie presenti
nelle quali esso ed i suoi vivono ne considera
e prevede le maggiori nelle quali la sua povera famiglia
dovrà cadere cessando esso di vivere / spazio di vento
e spazio di pioggia /
— non ci sono anime né persone per continuare infine
a mentire — steso nell'erba — post occasum — j'entendis
des voix /
laonde supplica umilmente la vostra real clemenza
a volersi degnare con suo real ordine di conferire
la futura sostituzione della mentovata catedra
in persona di detto suo figliuolo — né pubblicato
né perseguito — controcorrente / in contrasto
col tempo suo —
e ci sarebbe stato il grigio lucente dei pioppi
e delle nuvole sul viale — que je voudrais être vraiment —
acciocché la sua famiglia dopo la sua mancanza
possa almeno avere un qualche ricovero donde
in qualche maniera possa tener da sé lontana
una brutta e vergognosa povertà
                  nella quale certamente /
anderà a cadere — perché noi restiamo qui fino al mattino
— nuvola su nuvola — per strada /
solo dalle finestre dei gerolomini viene l'odore
dei gelsomini reali — au dessous:

of the body — that certain images form in the mind
there to remain — accompanied by and together with the strongest
such are those of the soul that have reduced him
to a state quite unfit for life —
                        no longer able
to drag his tired and almost crumbling body
in which condition he has seen the necessity to substitute
temporarily in his place in the chair of rhetoric
his son who — nigra absconditur umbra —
for many years has taken on the weight of this office
with some satisfaction to the public — une nuit entière
— il devait rester dans l'ombre — pour que je puisse lire
ma chance parmi les étoiles /
                — to remain or to define —
of which should be proof enough maintaining
the same competitions or the same interviews with the young
which he supplicatingly used to have and since he already
sees himself in declining age and from the present hardships
under which he and his family live he considers
and foresees the straits into which his poor family
must fall he ceasing to live / space of wind
and space of rain /
— at last there are neither souls nor persons to keep
lying — stretched out in the grass — post occasum — j'entendis
des voix /
whence he humbly prays your royal clemency
to deign with his royal order to confer
the future substitution of the aforementioned chair
in the person of said son — neither published
nor pursued — against the grain / in contrast
with his time —
and there would have been the lucid gray of poplars
and of clouds along the avenue — que je voudrais être vraiment —
so that his family after his departure
may at least have some shelter whence
they may keep from themselves in some way
an ugly and embarrassing poverty
                        into which they will
certainly fall — because we stay here until morning
— cloud upon cloud — along the street /
only from the windows of the jeromians comes the scent
of royal jasmine — au dessous:

                    kore nel campo dei melograni —
un volto in ombra come nel presagio e nelle voci — latet
in tenebris — sommerso / l'ora quieta — luce di crepuscolo
che cade — l'ora dei desideri tranquilli /
                                            la bellezza è qui
in questa piazza — nel limbo — seduti sui gradini —
in attesa — ancora in attesa della notte

Firenze, ottobre 1984

                    kore in the pomegranate field —
a face in shadow as in the omen and the voices — latet
in tenebris — submerged / the quiet hour — dusk light
that falls — the hour of calm desires /
                                beauty is here
in this piazza — in limbo — seated on the steps —
waiting — waiting still for the night

Florence, October 1984

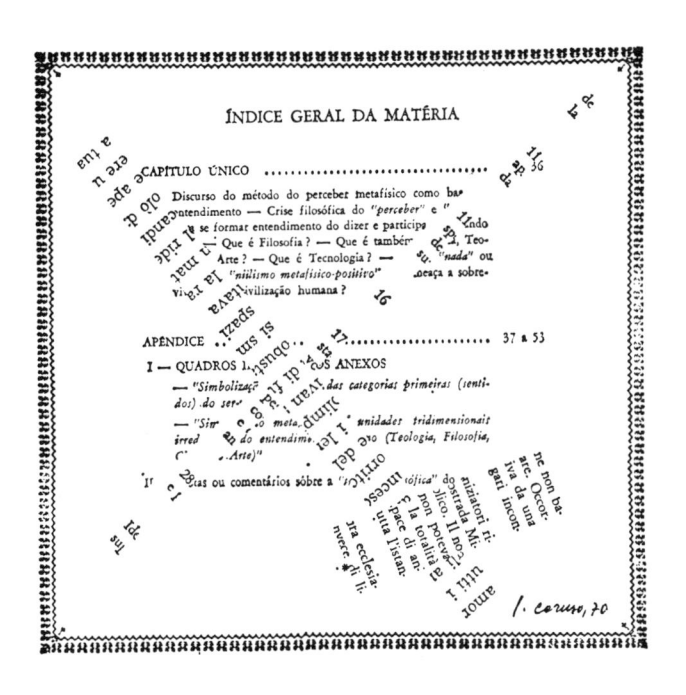

PER SERVIRE ALL'HISTORIA
parte I − l'ammonizione

mnene o catarsi: un triste mestiere: poeta
indovino traghettatore d'anime/ in ogni caso
un vago psicopompo − un messagero
ma senza il facile dono dell'improvvisazione
: lapsus e avvento per fili e termini alti/
ci voleva la morte come presenza
che così bene asseconda il ricordo
o l'iperbole ambigua del proscenio :
una livida premonizione nello scorrere dell'acqua
: il suo lucore anche : ma silenzioso − la fatica
della citazione sullo schermo o sulla pagina bianca :
gravida di sciagure e di conseguenze :
ci sarà un mutamento : è tutto scritto :
andando verso il sud −una figura che prevale
: sarò un attore un sensitivo un re sulla scena
o il principe amleto in viaggio verso citera :
in incognito certo : e anonimo nella nuova dimora
: altro non mi riesce di sapere − distratto
da un allarme concitato : e intravvedo ancòra
in mimesi bellissime camelie : muri screpolati :
che fioriscono nei vasi : sofferenti −
e dev'essere quello che è : rapporti stabiliti
nel trapianto del giorno con presenze incongrue
e atmosfere stremate in quello splendido giardino
nel giardino dei melangoli/

sarò giuditta o oloferne − vittima o vergine
dei profumi : appena sopra la fascia dipinta
con tutte le varietà dei marmi : che imitano il fuoco
: masse di silenzio : un gesto fermo nell'arco
di pietra sulla porta : l'amaro del distacco :
in un'opera del periodo giovanile : il luminismo
di un meriggio atteso:

la serie delle rose il gelsomino
la felicità il fiore dell'arancio
la violetta e la vaniglia
le spezie la pantera d'oro
il chiodo di garofano ed il tarlo
la canfora il sandalo ed il cedro

TO SERVE HISTORY

part I — the admonition

mnene or catharsis: a sad business: poet
diviner ferryman of souls/ in any case
a vague psychopomp — a messenger
but without the easy gift of improvisation
: lapse and adventitiousness for high wires and terminology/
death was needed as a presence
that so well seconds the memory
or the ambiguous hyperbole of the proscenium :
a livid premonition in the running of water
: even its splendor : but silent — the effort
of quotation on the screen or on the blank page :
pregnant with calamities and consequences :
there will be a change : it is all written :
heading toward the south — a prevailing figure
: I will be an actor a medium a king on the stage
or prince hamlet on a trip to cythera :
incognito of course : and anonymous in my new abode
: more I am not able to know — distracted
by an agitated alarm : and I still catch a glimpse
in mimesis of beautiful camelias : cracked walls:
that flower in vases : suffering —
and it must be what it is : relationships established
in the transplant of the day with incongruous presences
and extreme atmospheres in that splendid garden
in the garden of bitter oranges /

I will be judith or holofernes — victim or virgin
of perfumes : just above the band painted
with all varieties of marble : that imitate fire
: masses of silence : a still gesture in the arc
of stone above the door : the bitterness of detachment :
in a work of the youthful period: the illuminism
of awaited noon :

the series of roses the jasmine
the felicity the orange blossom
the violet and the vanilla
the spices the gold panther
the clove and the wood worm
the camphor the sandalwood and the cedar

l'incenso e la lavanda
la menta l'anice la mandorla
i frutti inclusi la mela la ciliegia e la cotogna
il muschio l'ambra e l'ambragrigia
e soprattutto il fuoco che nasce dalla pietra
: una scala per comprendere posta al centro
del campo:: un'insegna sul davanti :
immagine corrosa che non si lascia interpretare
: senza labbra né occhi : che non guarda :
repertorio o anagrafe che esprime la condanna
che è al fondo del tutto :

e venere riappare nella luce / *phaino* :
che sta per sembrare indicare mostrarsi /
maestra di sottili inganni : guardati da lei
: e si vede un abbandono del luogo prescelto
poi : procedere alla cura : inserire intervalli
e scarti simultanei — l'armonia della mano che
accarezza ed esplode in un giubilo imprevisto
: e piano risvanisce :

ci ha il colore che ci ha il ricordo
il colore del glicine stanco che matura
e sbiadisce nella luce : giardino di adone
: breve illusione : dove venere impura dà pianto
ai suoi e oscilla e deforma la nostra infedeltà :
rovina colui che ama e adora invece i detriti
trasognati di una città che s'indovina :
più vasta : organizzata : non di noi singoli :
col suo cielo limpido che accompagna
e immobilizza nel tempo che è dannato :
violento : ma anche vano — la cura crescente :
destinata alla proiezione : che distrugge
e rassicura :

: *glukys* vuol dire dolce — un segno chiaro —
vergine o venere la sua insegna nel dipinto
non è che fuoco liquido — luce coperta di sangue
amore preso a caso nel cortile del tempio —
fonemi elementari : lamenti : frammenti che vibrano
pieni di pulviscolo — certo virati in rosso
nella stampa — alba o tramonto dalla nave :
richiamo del cuore : fogliame secco e strame :
grumi di respiro e su tutto un gran senso

the incense and the lavender
the mint the anise the almond
the fruits included the apple the cherry and the quince
the moss the amber and the ambergris
and above all the fire that is born from the rock
: a ladder to comprehend placed in the center
of the field : an insignia on the front :
corroded image that does not allow interpretation
: without lips or eyes : that does not look :
directory or registry that expresses the condemnation
at the bottom of everything :

and venus reappears in the light / *phaino* :
that stands for resembling indicating showing /
mistress of subtle deceit : watch out for her
: and we see an abandoning of the chosen place
then : going on to the cure : putting in pauses
and simultaneous sidestepping — the harmony of the hand that
caresses and explodes in a sudden joy
: and slowly vanishes again :

it has the color that recollection has
the color of tired wisteria that ripens
and fades in the light : garden of adonis
: brief illusion : where impure venus cries
over hers and twists and deforms our infidelity :
ruins him who loves and adores instead the rubble
daydreamed of a city which we divine :
vaster : organized : not singly ours :
with its clear sky which in time
waits upon and immobilizes the damned :
violent : but even vain — the growing cure :
destined for projection : that destroys
and reassures :

: *glukys* means sweet — a clear sign —
virgin or venus her insignia in the painting
is nothing but liquid fire — light covered with blood
love taken by chance in the temple courtyard —
elementary phonemes : laments : fragments that vibrate
full of dust — certainly pushed towards red
in the print — dawn or dusk from the ship :
call from the heart : dry foliage and straw :
clots of breathing and over everything the strong sense

del corpo che ricopre la città :
con le sue porte torri e campanali — in basso
figure in scala pensano distratte da altre cose
: un'antigone muta di lato grida al fuoco — *pyros*
che davvero purifica e accende sogni
o solo consuma con semplicità con innocenza
e abbatte pensieri che sorgono da soli all'improvviso
nel dolore del giorno : che fu pieno di luce :
lungo : insolitamente chiaro :
sono io quel telemaco
che partì per pylos alla ricerca del padre e guarda
il fiume la terra il porto dell'arrivo :

segni ripresi e i semi e i seni — gli effetti secondari
: gli incontri parietali : la traccia che permane
nel lucore dello strangolo — gli arcani :
enigmi e frammenti che cerco di ordinare :
la ferita dell'ombra : la linea e i costrutti
del fuoco per chiedere clemenza e generare
un abbandono una rinuncia : espiazione volontaria
: ombre racchiuse che in sciame vanno incontro
ad ore vuote di presenza /
ore di rassegnazione e di risentimento e
leggi l'apocalisse dell'intonaco : i cretti chiari
: la sua rottura prudenziale anche : volontà ipocrita
di salvazione e strategia di migrazione delle anime
plasmata a riconquista dell'origine :

sarà un viaggio a ritroso : lemmi note e
panglosse in anatema — pubis stremato
perforato vinto alla fine :
morto e aperto tuttavia
ad un nuovo ciclo esponenziale : e all'opera dell'acqua
: l'asserto e lo sconcerto della lotta :
non richiesta : dal respiro corto : non rigenerabile
: registro dell'attesa infedele : historia persa
nel fraseggio del sangue : che per troppo amore
si consuma nella sua scoperta : camera terrifica
: fine intravista : fuga /
dove il nulla della vita scivola nel lago
delle acque primigenie che pure abbiamo offeso
con la disperazione della nostra profezia

Citera, estate 1985

of the body that covers the city :
with its doors towers and campaniles — below
figures to scale think distractedly of other things
: a mute antigone on the side screams at the fire — *pyros*
that truly purifies and lights up dreams
or only consumes with simplicity with innocence
and abates thoughts that surge suddenly by themselves
in the pain of day : which was full of light :
long : unusually clear :
I am that telemachus
who left for pylos in search of his father and watches
the river the land the port of arrival :

recovered signs and the seeds and the breasts — the secondary effects
: the parietal encounters : the trace which lasts
in the splendor of the strangling — the arcanes :
enigmas and fragments I seek to put in order :
the shadow's wound : the outlines and the constructions
of fire to ask for clemency and generate
an abandon a renunciation : voluntary expiation
: enclosed shadows going in swarms against
hours empty of presence /
hours of resignation and of resentment and
read the apocalypse on the plaster : the clear cracks
: its rupture even cautious : hypocritical will
for salvation and strategy of souls' migration
fashioned for a reconquest of our origins :

it will be a backward voyage : rubric notes and
general glosses in anathema — pubis exhausted
perforated vanquished at the end :
dead and open all the same
to a new exponential cycle : and to the work of the water
: the assertion and the disconcertedness of the struggle :
unasked for : from a short breath : unregenerative
record of the faithless waiting : history lost
in the phrasing of the blood : which from too much love
consumes itself in its own discovery : terrific chamber
: foreseen ending : flight /
where the nothingness of life slips into the lake
of primordial waters which we have yet offended
with the desperation of our prophecy

Cythera, summer 1985

UN APRILE DIPINTO — lezione di metodo

(per s.)
a Luciano Anceschi

era aprile nei tuoi occhi — ferma nell'immagine
leggera sul bordo del chiostro alla certosa —
aprile che ritorna negli affreschi della volta
e le lunette delle porte : un racconto continuo
con figure chiare in movimento che si affacciano
dalle nuvole dipinte in lontananza — nel silenzio
: allusione della morte :
      ritmo incantatorio :
parole sconosciute che si intrecciano : metamorfosi
obbligata : l'erotismo sottile dell'attesa :
solo un viso in ombra ricorda il trionfo del
nulla e la città che si stende con le sue cupole
dipinte in primo piano —
       in alto l'ansia si placa
nel volo degli angeli inquieti : nello stupore
che sale dalla strada o nel drappeggio rosso — scala
dell'essere o fondale di teatro —

      e aprile passa
sui teschi di marmo del giardino e riempie
le mattine — coppa irrigatoria che bagna i tuoi
capelli neri e riverbera voci e facce di
bambini —
   sarà facile guardare indietro da finte
architetture e definire il compito dell'identità
: le controversie di straluscio — il suo incanto
anche e il serpe e il flusso e il fulmine lontano :
la catastrofe che scende lungo le crepe del soffitto
— e aprile brucia e rigenera i contorni della vita
e traluce nell'avventura del colore —
       ma solo
nel fluire dell'istante o dell'amore : nella penombra
della stanza : i tuoi sorrisi : dove l'attimo trasale
e ridiscende verso il centro ed altre qualità e
impressioni che non sapresti dire —

ore desolate : ore di polvere e tempo sospeso —
e aprile avanza dal mare sulle pietre di tufo e
sul canneto superstite nella passeggiata del priore :

A PAINTED APRIL — *lesson in methodology*

(for s.)
to Luciano Anceschi

it was april in your eyes — firm in the delicate
image at the edge of the cloister at the certosa —
april that returns in frescoes on the vault
and the lunettes on doors : a continual story
with clear figures in motion who show forth
from the clouds painted in the distance — in silence
: allusion to death :
                  incantatory rhythm :
unknown words that twist together : obliged
metamorphosis : the subtle eroticism of waiting :
only a face in shadow recalls the triumph of
nothing and the city stretching out with its cupolas
painted in the foreground —
                            on high anxiety slackens
in the flight of uneasy angels : in the stupor
that rises from the road or in the red banner — stairway
of being or theatrical backdrop —

                     and april passes
on the marble bucranes in the garden and fills
the morning — irrigative cup wetting your
black hair and reverberating voices and faces of
children —
            it will be easy to look back from false
architectures and define the task of identity
: the controversies of motes in the sunlight — its incantation
even and the serpent and the flux and the far-off lightning:
the catastrophe descending through the cracks in the ceiling
— and april burns and regenerates the trimmings of life
and shines through in the adventure of color —
                                but only
in the flow of the instant or of love : in the penumbra
of the room : your smiles : where the moment leaps
and comes back down toward the center and other qualities and
impressions I wouldn't know how to speak of —

desolate hours : hours of dust and time suspended —
and april advances from the sea over tufa rock and
the surviving reeds in the prior's walk :

tocca l'essenza e ricomincia il ciclo :
                              l'anno insoluto
e si riflette nelle camelie pallide e nella
parietaria del cortile — dio della luce timida
in costante epifania che porta la morte ed è
nascita e luce e moltiplica l'apparenza delle vite
— chiuderò gli occhi sull'orrore di una piazza chiara
del sud aperta da una parte —
                       voci che si inseguono :
chi è colei che passa e raccoglie petali caduti e
fiori e non risponde : muta al richiamo :
come un sigillo del cuore : portatrice di pace :
                         : segno originario che
ricomincia da capo sempre : un sogno costruito
un gesto una perdita o confidenze d'ombra :
in luogo estraneo : *peribolos* — è il recinto
del tempio — dove il dio disegna la ferita che
è *hybris* senza margini e non si arresta —

                                        ore
sacre nell'attitudine e nel rischio della luce
: indice dei nomi o un elenco in appendice —
luce calcinata : che assomiglia dicevi con
gesto prezioso della mano a una piazza lontana
— s'è levato il vento — non possiamo più stare qui
: sguardi indifferenti : un viso strano o parole
che servono a nascondere :
                       fuggirò l'abbraccio
delle gran madri o il mistero di kore nell'aprile
improvviso che trascrive il gesto sulla scena
mi ricaccerà indietro in quella sala dove
si accresce il lutto primigenio : *vita vel sorte sua*
ma è lectio incerta —

                  abbiamo guardato la tenebra
senza fine la paura dell'amore e la distruzione
dell'orgasmo prima che la speranza del mattino
servisse a riscattarlo — e certo è senza macchia : e
ci si potrebbe anche amare nell'inedia del ricordo
o nell'emozione degli incastri :
                           dimenticherò
tutto in un abbraccio differito : et non v'ho
scripto per non m'esser fermo in nessun luogo

it touches the essence and starts the cycle once more:
                                    the year unresolved
and reflected in the pale camelias and the
parietaria in the courtyard — god of timid light
in constant epiphany that brings death and is
birth and light and multiplies the appearance of our lives
— I will close my eyes on the horror of a bright piazza
in the south open at one end —
                        voices that follow each other:
who is with her that passes and gathers fallen petals and
flowers and does not answer : mute to the call :
like a seal on the heart : bearer of peace :
                    : original sign which
always begins anew : a dream constructed
a gesture a loss or shadowy confidences :
in a foreign place : *peribolos* — is the enclosure
of the temple — where the god designs the wound that
is *hybris* without borders and unchecked —

                            hours
sacred in the attitude and the risk of light
: index of names or a list appended —
chalky light : that resembles you were saying with
precious gesture of your hand a far away piazza
— the wind came up — we cannot stay here any longer
: indifferent glances : a strange face or words
which serve to hide :
                I will flee the embrace
of the great mothers or the mystery of kore in the sudden
april that transcribes the gesture on the scene
will drive me back into that room where
the primordial mourning grows; *vita vel sorte sua*
but it's an uncertain reading —

                    we have watched the darkness
without end the fear of love and the destruction
of orgasm before the hope of morning
served to redeem it — and surely it is without stain : and
we might also love in the bloodless recollection
or in the emotions of puzzles :
                    I will forget
it all in a deferred embrace : and I haven't
written thee for that I have never tarried in any place

[155]

: una presenza — toccare il mare con la mano : un
rito un urlo spento grido inafferrabile — eraclito
al frammento 119 : la sibilla con bocca di follia
dà suono a parole che non hanno sorriso né bellezza
né profumo e giunge al di là di mille anni
per il dio che é in lei : e vincere i pensieri
— la perdita nell'enfasi :

            e sempre *tà erotikà* è
solo l'amore del bello — una felicità improvvisa —
ma il termine non appare altrove attestato —
                                      frammenti
di una pagina sacrificale — vessillo di scrittura
immaginaria — impeto mancato che distrugge limiti e
possesso — sospiro breve : ferita aperta i canti
per un cuore afflitto — poco più di un'immagine
nella lettera dell'imperatore — intravista nel ricordo
o nella profezia : che occulta il nome :
                              e possano
perire i tessitori di storie :
                    i malvagi che seminano
parole e leggende odiose :
                    un'irruzione inattesa :
la tua ombra e il gelo che brucia le camelie e
gli alberi fioriti : squarcio e abbandono che rivela :
tu non lo puoi dire o indovinare : presa nell'impatto
di certe semideserte sale nel pomeriggio sospeso : e
ancora disegni di marmi commessi con motivi floreali :
che non nascono da un impeto fantastico ma da un'
estrema pazienza — e solo per invidia immaginano
l'inesistente :

           pséphos è detto di chi vive felicemente
: non ancora estinto — o il contrario ? — e per primo
il misfatto colpisce chi lo trama — tarsie regolari
in antitesi con le figure al centro : i racemi gli
stucchi e le volute — verso l'uscita — un ammasso
di frante immagini — maledizione senza motivo :
                                             e aprile
mescola nell'indistinto fuoco e acqua — voci e luoghi
sparisce nelle similitudini o nella disposizione
e solo crea una disperazione più grande :
                                      muta l'acqua

: a presence — touch the sea with your hand : a
rite a spent scream an untouchable cry — heraclitus
in fragment 119 : the sybil with her mouth of madness
gives cry to words that have no smile nor beauty
nor perfume and reaches beyond a thousand years
for the god who is in her : and to win thoughts
— the loss in bombast :

                and always *tà erotika* is
only the love of the beautiful — a sudden happiness —
but the term appears nowhere else attested —
                                  fragments
of a sacrificial page — ensign of an imaginary
writing — failed impetus that destroys limits and
possession — brief sigh : open wound the songs
for an afflicted heart — little more than an image
in the emperor's letter — glimpsed in recollection
or in prophecy : which hides the name :
                                  and may
the weavers of stories perish :
                      the wicked who sow
words and hateful legends :
                  a sudden eruption :
your shadow and the frost that burns the camelias and
the flowering trees : tear and abandon that reveals :
you cannot say or guess : captured in the impact
of certain semideserted rooms in the suspended afternoon : and
still designs of marble inlaid with floral motives :
which are not born of a fantastic impetus but from an
extreme patience — and only out of envy they imagine
the non-existent :

                psephos is said of who lives happily
: not yet extinct — or the contrary? — and the crime
strikes first who plots it — regular inlay
against figures in the center : the plaster branches the
stucco figures and scroll work — towards the exit — a mass
of crushed images — malediction without motive :
                                    and april
mixes fire and water in the yet indistinct — voices and places
vanishes in the likenesses or in the disposition
and only creates a greater desperation :
                            changes the water

del mare apre le sorgenti sfiora le acque abissali
lacera il velo della dea : e spezza l'anima in pena
che cammina accanto a noi — così tanta moltitudine
di gente che non si può andare per le strade :
             è stato
scritto : con poca perizia tecnica : e aveva fatto
fissare il marmo sottile direttamente sul battuto
mediante pece e cera greca : una cifra : una mappa
involontaria : impulsi causati da afflizione :
             e
raffigurò le albe immotivate — la loro morte —
senza dolore : che derivano da *oarizein* : essere
in intimità :
    malgrado i crolli e le rovine :

of the sea opens the springs skims over the abysmal waters
splits the veil of the goddess : and shatters the soul in pain
walking alongside us — so many multitudes
of people we cannot pass through the streets :
                                        it was
written : with little technical skill : and had the thin
marble fixed right to the earthen floor
by means of tar and Greek wax : a cipher : an involuntary
map : impulses caused by affliction :
                        and
I will portray the unjustified dawns — their death —
without pain : that derive from *oarizein* : to be
in intimacy :
            in spite of the crumbling and the ruins

above: GL'OSSA (1978) by Luciano Caruso.

FOREST BEYOND NATURE was designed by John McBride. Composition at PICOT PRODUCTIONS by Paul Cuneo (who can only wonder at the sheer plentitude involved in this project of *exhausting* Italian).
Printed in the USA.

Other translations from the Italian by Paul Vangelisti published by Red Hill Press

Franco Beltrametti: *Another Earthquake* (1976)
Corrado Costa: *Our Positions* (1975)
       The Complete Films of Corrado Costa (1983)
Giulia Niccolai: *Substitution* (1975)
Antonio Porta: *as if it were a rhythm* (1978)
       Invasions: Selected Poems (1986)
Rocco Scotellaro: *The sky with its mouth wide open* (1976)
Vittorio Sereni: *Sixteen Poems* (1971)
       Algerian Diary (1985)
Adriano Spatola: *Majakovskiiiiiij* (1975)
       Zeroglyphics (1977)
       Various Devices (1978)

Italian Poetry, 1960 —1980: from Neo to Post Avant-garde, edited by Adriano Spatola & Paul Vangelisti. Some 77 visual & linear poets from Accame to Xerra. "In Italian poetry of the last 20 years, direct language is not always spoken language, and indirect language is not always that of the written word." (1982)

The Red Hill Press
PO BOX 2853
San Francisco CA 94126